SMALL ENGINE CARE & REPAIR

A step-by-step guide to maintaining your small engine

CREATIVE
PUBLISHING
international

CHANHASSEN, MINNESOTA

Small Engine Care & Repair

Created by: The Editors of Creative Publishing international, Inc., in cooperation with Briggs & Stratton Corporation.

Post Office Box 702
Milwaukee, WI 53201-0702
1-800-233-3723
www.briggsandstratton.com
www.tuneupmonth.com

Vice President, Marketing: William Reitman
Director of Sales, Distribution Sales &
  Customer Support Division: Timothy J. Schreiber
Manager of Service Marketing: Cherie R. Burns
National Retail Sales Manager: Garry Rainey
Technical Editor, Product Service Trainer, Customer Education
  Department Briggs & Stratton: Don Koloski
Marketing Coordinator: Synoilva Shaw
Technical Service Representative: Mark Warnke

18705 Lake Drive East
Chanhassen, MN 55317
1-800-328-3895
www.creativepub.com

President: Michael Eleftheriou
Vice President, Publisher: Linda Ball
Vice President, Retail Sales: Kevin Haas
Vice President, Custom Services: Karen Kreiger

Author: Daniel London
Creative Director: Jim Oldsberg
Managing Editors: Jennifer Caliandro, Michelle Skudlarek
Executive Editor: Bryan Trandem
Illustrators: Jan Boer, Derek Brigham
Mac Production Artists: Patricia Kleffman, Dave McCullough
Writers/Editors: Clayton Bennett, Karl Larson, Steve Waryan
Technical Photo Editors: Scott Christenson, Joel Schmarje,
  Greg Wallace
Copy Editors: Janice Cauley, Tracy Stanley
Project Manager: Christy Balfanz

Director Production Services & Photography: Kim Gerber
Studio Services Manager: Jeanette Moss McCurdy
Photographers: Tate Carlson, Jamey Mauk, Charles Nields
Models: Jerri Farris, Michelle Skudlarek
Technical Editors: Don Koloski, Ken Warwick,

Special thanks to Erv's Lawnmower Repair and
Wisconsin Magneto, Inc.

Printed on American paper by
  R.R. Donnelley
10 9 8 7 6 5 4 3 2

Contents

Introduction — 4
  History of small engine — 6
  Small engine appli — 8
  Tools — 10
  Safety — 12

Understanding small engines — 14
  Engine components & their function — 15
  Parts of the small engine — 16
  Compression system — 20
  Fuel system — 24
  Ignition system — 26
  Lubrication & cooling system — 28
  Governor system — 30
  Braking system — 32
  Electrical system — 34

Tune-up — 36
  March is tune-up month — 37
  Four simple steps — 38
  Maintenance kits — 39
  Maintenance Mate and Minder — 40
  Web sites — 41

Maintenance — 42
  Regular maintenance schedule — 43
  Checking & changing oil — 46
  Servicing spark plugs — 50
  Servicing air cleaners — 52
  Additional maintenance — 56

Basic repair — 58
  Troubleshooting — 60
  Inspecting & changing the muffler — 62
  Removing debris — 66
  Servicing the fuel tank — 70
  Servicing the fuel filter — 72
  Servicing the fuel pump — 74
  Adjusting the carburetor — 76
  Adjusting the governor — 80
  Replacing the rewind — 86

Advanced repair — 88
  Overhauling the carburetor — 90
  Inspecting the flywheel & key — 98
  Replacing the ignition — 100
  Testing the electrical system — 104
  Removing carbon deposits — 108
  Servicing the valves — 112
  Servicing the brake — 122

Additional tools, parts & supplies — 128

Maintenance log — 132

Index — 140

INTRODUCTION

Small engines have improved the quality of our lives by providing portable power where and when it is needed. And as our needs have grown, so has small engine use. Small engines power lawn mowers and other equipment that is making many yard chores easier than ever. They also power equipment for painting, washing, masonry and an array of other outdoor home projects. Sales and rentals of these types of equipment increase each year.

Briggs & Stratton's edge

Briggs & Stratton has been a major force behind the explosion in small engine popularity. This quintessential American company builds more than two-thirds of all lawn mower engines and is a major producer of four-stroke small engines for almost every application. You may find many brands of mowers, tractors and other equipment at your power equipment retailer. Look closely: chances are good the engines are built by Briggs & Stratton. Retailers like to point this out because the name stands for quality and experience.

Briggs & Stratton's knowledge and expertise is second to none. When you learn from Briggs & Stratton technicians, you're learning from the company that has set the industry standard for decades.

You're also developing skills that apply to more than lawn equipment. With the information in this book, you can maintain and repair small engines on a variety of power equipment—from generators and pressure washers, to hydraulic lifts. You'll even understand many of the principles of car engines—although car engine repair is considerably more complex and requires specialized training.

Organization of the book

This book takes you through dozens of projects, based on the most widely used small engine designs. You can find the step-by-step directions for your project in the Table of Contents (page 3) or by turning to one of the three sections listed below.
- "Maintenance" (pages 37 to 57) offers a convenient schedule and checklist for inspecting and changing the oil, spark plugs and filters.
- "Basic Repair" (pages 58 to 87) guides you through troubleshooting and repair of the most common problems.
- "Advanced Repair" (pages 88 to 127) covers engine problems that are a bit more complex. These projects require more time, but they're not difficult once you've handled a few basic repairs. Most important, these projects allow you to assess and treat long-term wear and tear; they can dramatically increase the power, reliability and life span of your engine.

Other benefits

Each section of the book offers safety, tool and shopping tips. You'll find descriptions of every engine part and a tool list for every project. Common replacement parts are pictured at the back of the book (pages 128 to 131).

Now, roll up your sleeves and get the satisfaction of repairing your own small engine.

WHERE TO FIND US

You never have to look far to find Briggs & Stratton support and service for your small engine. Consult your **Yellow Pages** under "Engines-Gasoline," "Gasoline-Engines," "Lawn Mowers" or similar categories. There are over 30,000 Briggs & Stratton authorized service dealers worldwide who provide quality service.

You can also contact **Briggs & Stratton Customer Service** by phone at 1-800-233-3723, or on the Internet at www.briggsandstratton.com or www.tuneupmonth.com.

HISTORY OF SMALL ENGINES

The founders of the company that would bear their name, Harry Stratton and Steve Briggs, take a spin on the Flyer, a vehicle propelled by a 2-HP Model D Motor Wheel. The Flyer, priced between $145 and $225, was one of the most inexpensive cars designed for road use. Approximately 2,000 were made between 1920 and 1923.

You may think of the small engine in your lawn mower or tiller as a 20th-century American invention. In fact, it's based on European designs that were around long before the United States.

The first internal combustion engines were large, clunky apparatuses that mimicked early firearms. In the first internal combustion engine, designed by a Dutchman in 1680, gunpowder exploded to drive a slug through a tube, much as it drove shot down the barrel of a musket. In modern small engines, a burning mixture of air and fuel (usually gasoline) has replaced gunpowder, offering the advantage of more efficient combustion. But the principles are much the same.

A 17th-century Scotsman added two other features: valves, which allow a piston to work in two directions; and a governor, to keep engine speed constant. Both are integral to the design of today's small engine.

The gasoline-powered washing machine brought big-city convenience to rural areas that were not yet wired for electricity.

A dynamic team enters the business

In the 1920s, Briggs & Stratton became a major force in the emerging industry. Harry Stratton and Steve Briggs—a brilliant engineer and a savvy businessman—designed and built the Model P, a small engine that could power reel-type lawn mowers, garden tractors, air compressors and generators. Mass production of the Model P sent Briggs & Stratton on its way to becoming synonymous with small engine production.

Uses for the Model P were wide ranging, but the enormous success of this single-horsepower wonder owed much to an emerging market for gasoline-powered washing machines. Although electric washing machines were already available, millions of rural homes had no access to electricity. The Model P filled this void.

While the mainly cast-iron Model P was effective for stationary equipment, it was heavy and impractical for engine-powered mowing. It wasn't until 1953 that Briggs & Stratton introduced its first diecast aluminum engine, making engine-powered mowers lighter and easier to operate. Sales boomed. By 1967, the company had sold 50 million small engines.

Advances in design and your small engine

Refinements like flywheel brakes, solid-state ignitions and electric starter motors have made small engines safer, cleaner-running and more reliable and practical each year. Those refinements continue at Briggs & Stratton, due to a long-standing commitment to research and development.

Today's small engines, such as the Briggs & Stratton Quantum® engines featured in this book, represent years of refinement of the same tried-and-true features found on the steam engine and on the Model P and other early small engines. On the following pages you'll learn more about the basic principles of internal combustion and the modern refinements on your small engine. Best of all, you'll learn how to get the most out of your small engine by maintaining and repairing it yourself.

1900: the early gasoline engine

After a century in which steam, gasoline and diesel battled for dominance as the engine fuel of choice, American-built automobiles of the early 1900s gave the gasoline engine a mystique all its own. Automobiles were still too expensive for most Americans, but they popularized the notion that engines could simplify daily life. Entrepreneurs hoping to build on this appeal began designing engines to power smaller, less expensive machines that could tap into the broader American market.

These innovators increased the range of a popular mode of transportation, the bicycle, by adding a wheel-mounted engine, and they made farm labor easier with self-propelled plows and other farm equipment. An explosion in small engine applications was around the corner.

Small engines can be used for fun as well as work. The 4-stroke Briggs & Stratton Raptor® engine on this go-kart is a mainstay of the small engine racing circuit.

SMALL ENGINE APPLICATIONS

The lawn tractor has changed the way many homeowners think about mowing. Owning a home with a large lawn no longer means hiring a gardener. A comfortable, powerful lawn tractor makes it possible to "do it yourself" and recoup the cost in just a few years. In cold climates, lawn tractors double as plows, making quick work of sidewalk or driveway snow clearing.

You don't have to look far to realize how popular the four-stroke small engine has become. There are millions of these engines on lawn mowers alone; nearly every homeowner owns one. But today, the term "small engines" means much more than walk-behind lawn mowers. Four-stroke small engines—they range from modest three-horsepower (HP) mower engines to 25-HP engines for tractors and other heavy-duty equipment—are found on tillers, wood chippers, garden tractors, compressors, generators and other products that growing numbers of homeowners and commercial users own and operate.

The affordability, low maintenance, and easy-to-use design of Briggs & Stratton engines have given owners the tools to tackle outdoor projects that once were too difficult and time-consuming. Small engines have also attracted many homeowners to ambitious hobbies, like gardening and do-it-yourself home improvement.

With a wood chipper, branches and other yard debris become a source of wood-chip mulch to place around trees, shrubs and flowers. Mulch protects plants and helps maintain soil moisture.

You may never purchase your own compactor, but an inexpensive rental unit allows you to build a professional-quality brick or stone patio.

Pressure washers are increasingly popular for washing the family car, driveway and patio. They're also ideal for washing decks and external walls in preparation for painting or staining.

A portable generator offers electrical power wherever you need it.

This gas-powered hydraulic lift, available for lease at many rental centers, lets you work at heights without a ladder. Many tasks once reserved for professionals can now be done by homeowners, thanks to small engines.

The 5-HP Briggs & Stratton engine on this tiller opens up lots of gardening possibilities. Few individuals have the time or patience to handle a large garden using only hand tools. With a tiller, you can turn topsoil in no time at all.

TOOLS

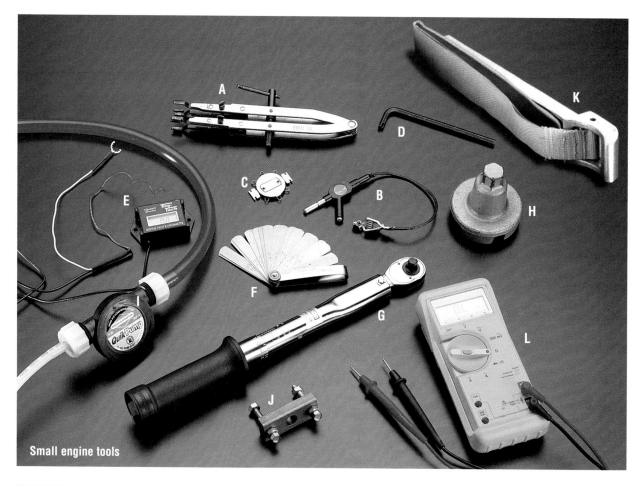

Small engine tools

The right tools make your maintenance and repair tasks easier and give you better results. Have these tools available:

Small engine tools

(A) Valve spring compressor
(B) Spark tester
(C) Spark plug gauge
(D) Tang bending tool
(E) Tachometer
(F) Feeler gauges
(G) Ratchet torque wrench
(H) Starter clutch wrench
(I) Oil evacuator pump
(J) Flywheel puller
(K) Flywheel strap wrench
(L) Multimeter

Use the correct tools for each job. Using other tools as substitutes can damage your engine and may create a safety hazard.

When buying tools, choose the highest quality you can afford. Well-made tools help you do a better job and will give you years of reliable service. For further guidance on

General-purpose tools

(A) Socket set
(B) Standard screwdriver
(C) Phillips screwdriver
(D) Parts cleaning brush
(E) Power drill
(F) Putty knife
(G) Shot-filled mallet
(H) Center punch
(I) Flat file
(J) Needlenose pliers
(K) Adjustable pliers
(L) Star-shaped driver set
(M) Standard pliers
(N) Adjustable wrench
(O) Wire cutters
(P) Baster
(Q) Fuel line crimper
(R) Combination wrenches
(S) Hex wrench set
(T) Locking pliers

tools, see "Additional Tools, Parts & Supplies," pages 128 to 131 (Also see service tools catalog *MS-8746*).

SAFETY

You can avoid a serious safety hazard—carbon monoxide (CO) accumulation—by working outdoors. CO is an odorless, tasteless, poisonous gas produced by burning gasoline and other fuels. A carbon monoxide detector can alert you to the presence of CO indoors before it reaches lethal levels.

Small engines must burn fuel and induce electricity. Each of these involves special safety considerations —so you need to observe the precautions for both. Keep the following rules in mind, and you will simplify the job of safely operating, maintaining and repairing your small engine.

Operating conditions

If you need to run an engine to test your maintenance or repair work:

• Never run an engine indoors.

• Turn off the engine before leaving the area—even for a few seconds.

• Do not operate the engine in dry grass or near combustible materi-

als, gasoline or other flammable liquids.

• Keep combustible materials away from the muffler.

• Avoid running an engine at high speeds or in excess of the manufacturer's specifications.

• Make sure the muffler is in place before starting the engine.

• Pull the starter cord slowly until you feel resistance, then pull rapidly to start; this helps prevent injury to your hand and arm.

• Do not crank the engine with the spark plug removed; if the engine is flooded, place the throttle in the FAST position and crank until the engine starts.

• To stop the engine, gradually reduce engine speed. Then, turn the key to OFF or move the controls to the OFF or STOP position.

• When operating equipment on unimproved land covered by grass or brush, install a spark arrester— designed to trap sparks discharged from the engine.

• Keep equipment flat on the ground when it is operating. Never tilt it at a sharp angle.

• Keep hands and feet away from moving or rotating parts on the engine or equipment.

Gasoline safety

The only place where engine fuel and sparks should interact is in the combustion chamber. To reduce fire hazards:

- Never light a match or other flammable material near an engine.
- Avoid using power tools or other equipment that generates sparks where fuel vapors may be present.
- Allow the engine to cool before removing the fuel cap or filling the tank.
- Replace a fuel line or fitting if it is leaky or cracked.
- Keep gasoline, solvents and other flammables out of reach of children. Store gasoline in UL®-approved non-spill containers. Label flammable materials containers clearly for quick identification.
- Never smoke while using, servicing or refueling an engine.

Safe maintenance

To make small engine maintenance and repair tasks easier and safer:

- Make sure you have ample work space, with easy access to the tools you need.
- Use the correct tools for each job.
- Keep an approved fire extinguisher in a familiar location near your work area.
- Learn engine shutoff procedures so you can respond quickly in an emergency.

FILLING THE FUEL TANK

Spilled or dripping fuel can cause harm to you, your equipment and the environment. You can reduce these occurrences by using a UL®-approved non-spill can for transporting fuel and refueling. When filling, place your fuel can or power equipment on the ground—away from appliances, heaters and other sources of flame or heat. Never fill your can or refuel your equipment while either one is inside a trunk or on a truck bed. During transport, fuel should be in a secure, upright position and tightly sealed. Provide ample ventilation to prevent fumes from building up in the passenger compartment or trunk, where static electricity could ignite gas fumes.

Briggs & Stratton's Smart-Fill® Fuel Can is designed to prevent spills, overfills and the escape of harmful emissions.

- Disengage the cutting blade, wheels or other equipment, if possible, before starting the engine.
- Disconnect the spark plug wire to prevent accidental starting when you are servicing the engine.
- Always disconnect the wire from the negative terminal when servicing an electric starter motor.
- Check that a spark plug or spark plug tester is attached to the engine before cranking.
- Avoid contact with hot engine parts, such as the muffler, cylinder head or cooling fins.
- Never strike the flywheel with a hammer or hard object; it may cause the flywheel to shatter during operation.
- Make sure the air cleaner assembly and blower housing are in place before starting the engine.

SPARK PLUG SAFETY

Some engines use a stop contact to ground the spark plug and stop the engine. By pressing a lever, the operator creates contact between the spark plug terminal and the engine chassis, which stops the engine. A stop contact should ensure that the engine doesn't start accidentally. For complete protection, however, always disconnect the spark plug lead and secure it away from the plug during maintenance. This prevents the engine from starting even if the crankshaft is turned manually.

- Remove any fuel from the tank and close the fuel shutoff valve before transporting an engine.
- Use only the original manufacturer's replacement parts; any other parts may damage the engine and create safety hazards.
- Keep engine speed settings within manufacturer specifications. Higher speeds can ruin the engine.

Protecting your health

Fire, electric shock and asphyxiation are not the only dangers when working with small engines. Take care to avoid long-term or sudden injury to your eyes, ears, lungs, feet and back:

- Keep your feet, hands and clothing away from moving engine and equipment components.
- Use eye protection when you work with engines or power tools.
- Wear ear protection to reduce the risk of gradual hearing loss from exposure to engine noise.
- Wear a face mask, if required, when working with chemicals.
- Wear specially designed gloves to protect against heat, harmful chemicals and sharp objects.
- Wear safety shoes to protect against falling objects; safety shoes have soles that won't deteriorate when exposed to gasoline or oil.
- Use proper lifting techniques and seek help with heavy lifting.

UNDERSTANDING SMALL ENGINES

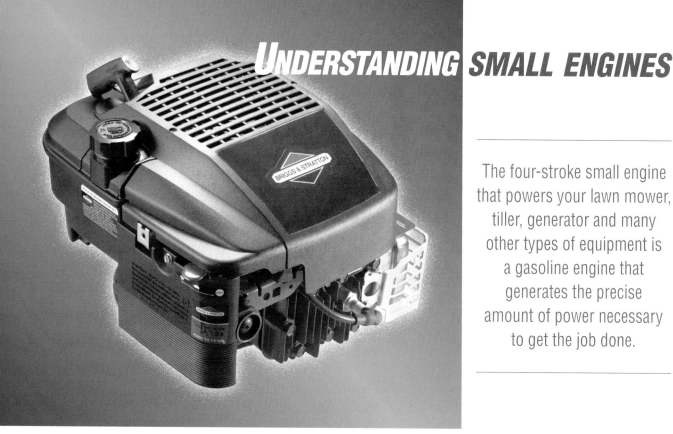

The four-stroke small engine that powers your lawn mower, tiller, generator and many other types of equipment is a gasoline engine that generates the precise amount of power necessary to get the job done.

The biggest difference between small engines and other types of engines is their small capacity and simplicity of design. Small engines generate very modest amounts of power—generally no more than 25 HP—compared to a typical family car (up to 200 HP). And a small engine's size makes it easier to maintain and repair.

Since small engines are designed for simple tasks like cutting grass and turning soil, their designs are fairly uncomplicated. Unlike cars and other vehicles that frequently accelerate, slow down or idle for long periods, small engines either run at constant speed or change speed slightly to handle modest changes in the "load," such as when a lawnmower hits a patch of thick grass.

Also, unlike car engines, small engines don't have to fit under a hood or make room for countless computers and other devices. This makes small engine parts easier to install, adjust and remove. You can reach most small engine parts with a few turns of a wrench.

Essentials of the four-stroke engine

Here, in its simplest form, is how a four-stroke engine works:

When you pull the rope, known as a **rewind cord,** or use your electric starter, precise amounts of fuel and filtered air mix in the **carburetor.** The mixture rushes into the engine to be compressed, ignited and burned in a controlled process known as internal combustion. Hot gases are produced. As the gases expand, they push a smooth, well-lubricated cylindrical component, known as the **piston.** The piston, in turn, drives the **crankshaft,** the arm that spins a blade or performs other work. Valves let air and fuel into the **combustion chamber** above the piston and allow spent gases to exit through the **muffler.**

The whole process involves four piston strokes (two up strokes and two down strokes, described on pages 22 to 23) and is designed to become self-sustaining from the time the engine starts until the moment it stops. Timed electrical surges cause the **spark plug** to fire repeatedly inside the combustion chamber, igniting each fresh supply of air and fuel and producing gases that continually drive the piston and crankshaft.

All the while, oil from the **crankcase** and air circulate to keep engine temperatures within an acceptable range, and a governor monitors changes in the workload and adjusts engine speed accordingly.

Five basic systems

There are five systems at work in every small engine: **fuel supply, compression, ignition, lubrication and cooling,** and **governor** (speed control). Each of these systems is explained in depth in the following pages.

Two other common systems are also discussed in detail. Some engine models—especially heavier-duty ones—may contain a starter motor, which requires an **electrical system** to charge the battery.

Most small engines sold in the past 10-15 years include a **braking system** as well. This is designed to protect you and others by stopping the engine quickly if you let go of the controls.

In short, five systems generate the power to spin a blade, turn a wheel or perform other work. Two others may be included for safety and convenience. The following pages will familiarize you with the major parts in these systems and the essentials of how they work.

Engine components and their function

Here's how the components in your engine interact (all of the components mentioned below are shown in detail on pages 16 to 19):

The *rewind cord* is pulled to start the combustion process. On some models, a starter motor replaces the rewind, drawing on battery power to start the engine.

Revolving *magnets* work in conjunction with the *ignition armature* and *spark plug* to produce a spark in the *combustion chamber.*

The *carburetor* draws in fuel from the fuel tank and outside air to form a combustible vapor that is fed into the combustion chamber.

Intake and exhaust valves open and close at precisely timed intervals to let air and fuel enter the engine and to let spent gases exit.

The *piston* is pushed through the *cylinder* by the force of expanding gases. The piston's motion causes the *crankshaft* to turn. Momentum then carries the piston back toward the top of the cylinder.

Oil stored in the *crankcase* circulates through the engine to lubricate key components like the piston and crankshaft

and to provide generalized cooling by drawing away heat from internal engine surfaces.

A *flywheel brake* and *stop switch* are included on engines for equipment such as mowers that require constant supervision. The two components are designed to stop the engine if you release the controls.

An *air vane* or *flyweights* monitor engine RPMs so the governor can maintain the selected engine speed.

Cooling fins help reduce engine temperatures when air circulates across the hottest engine surfaces.

This Briggs & Stratton Intek®
22-HP engine represents the
cutting edge in small engine design.
A compact "V-twin" design means two
overhead-valve cylinders can operate,
producing minimal vibration.

Parts of the Overhead valve (OHV) small engine – front view

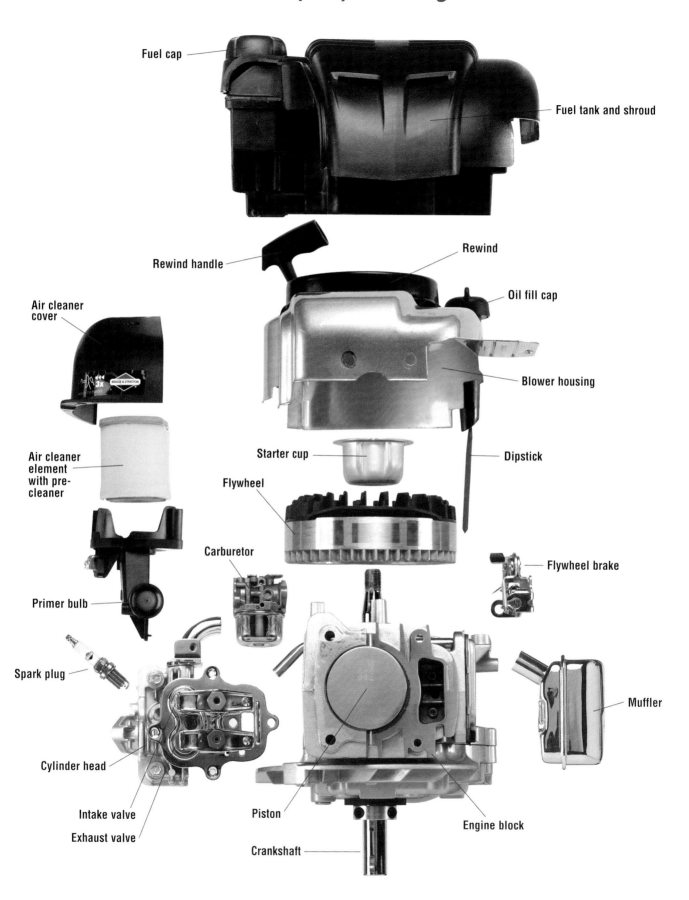

Fuel cap

Fuel tank and shroud

Rewind handle

Rewind

Oil fill cap

Air cleaner cover

Blower housing

Air cleaner element with pre-cleaner

Starter cup

Dipstick

Flywheel

Carburetor

Flywheel brake

Primer bulb

Spark plug

Muffler

Cylinder head

Intake valve

Piston

Engine block

Exhaust valve

Crankshaft

Parts of the Overhead valve (OHV) small engine – side view

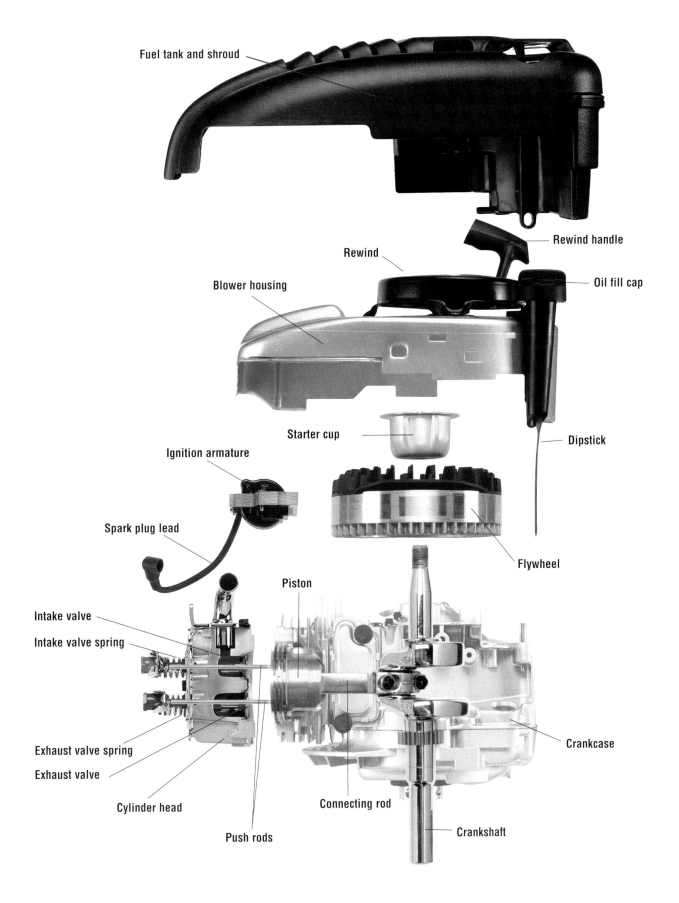

Fuel tank and shroud

Rewind handle

Rewind

Blower housing

Oil fill cap

Starter cup

Dipstick

Ignition armature

Spark plug lead

Flywheel

Piston

Intake valve

Intake valve spring

Exhaust valve spring

Exhaust valve

Crankcase

Cylinder head

Connecting rod

Push rods

Crankshaft

Parts of the small engine – front view

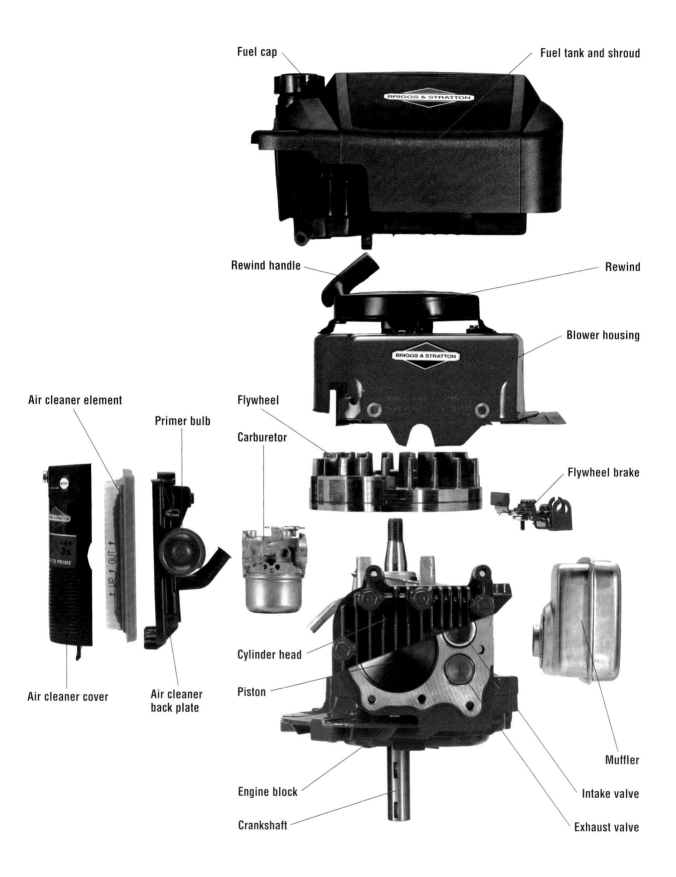

Fuel cap

Fuel tank and shroud

Rewind handle

Rewind

Blower housing

Air cleaner element

Flywheel

Primer bulb

Carburetor

Flywheel brake

Air cleaner cover

Air cleaner back plate

Cylinder head

Piston

Muffler

Engine block

Intake valve

Crankshaft

Exhaust valve

Parts of the small engine – side view

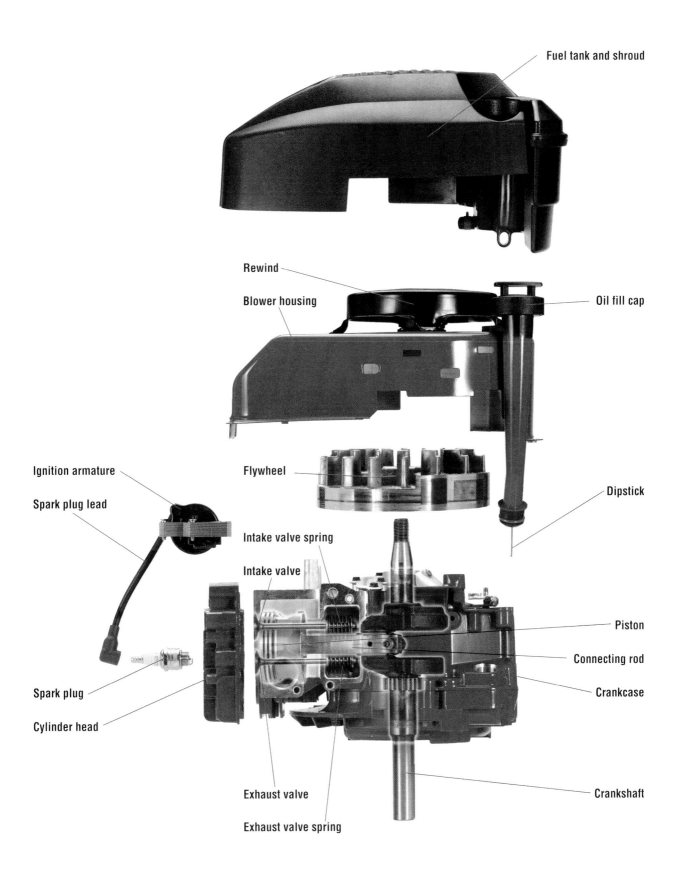

Fuel tank and shroud

Rewind

Blower housing

Oil fill cap

Ignition armature

Flywheel

Dipstick

Spark plug lead

Intake valve spring

Intake valve

Piston

Connecting rod

Crankcase

Spark plug

Cylinder head

Exhaust valve

Crankshaft

Exhaust valve spring

COMPRESSION SYSTEM

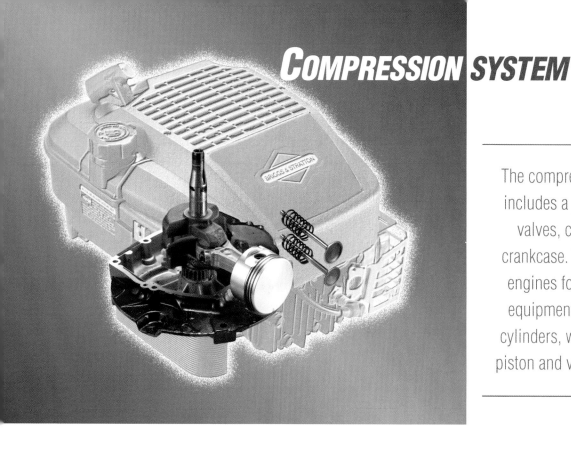

The compression system includes a piston, rings, valves, cylinder and crankcase. Twin-cylinder engines for heavy-duty equipment contain two cylinders, with a separate piston and valves for each.

The inventors of the first internal combustion engines discovered that fuel burns more efficiently if you compress it in a sealed chamber before burning it. Compression of the air-fuel mixture in the small engine begins as the ***intake valve*** closes. The trapped vapors are pushed toward the ***cylinder head*** by the ***piston*** and compressed into a space about one-sixth their original volume. The exact amount of compression is an indicator of an engine's efficiency. That's why a tightly sealed ***combustion chamber*** is so important for good engine performance.

Valves

Valves located in the combustion chamber let fuel vapors and air enter the cylinder and let exhaust gases exit at precisely timed intervals. A typical four-stroke cycle small engine contains one ***intake valve*** and one ***exhaust valve*** per cylinder.

Most small engines have one cylinder and use an L-head (or flathead) design. The valves are installed in a valve chamber next to the piston. Overhead valve (OHV) designs offer greater efficiency, however, and are increasingly popular with consumers. The valves are located in the cylinder head directly in line with the piston and are moved by pivoting ***rocker arms.***

Parts of the compression system

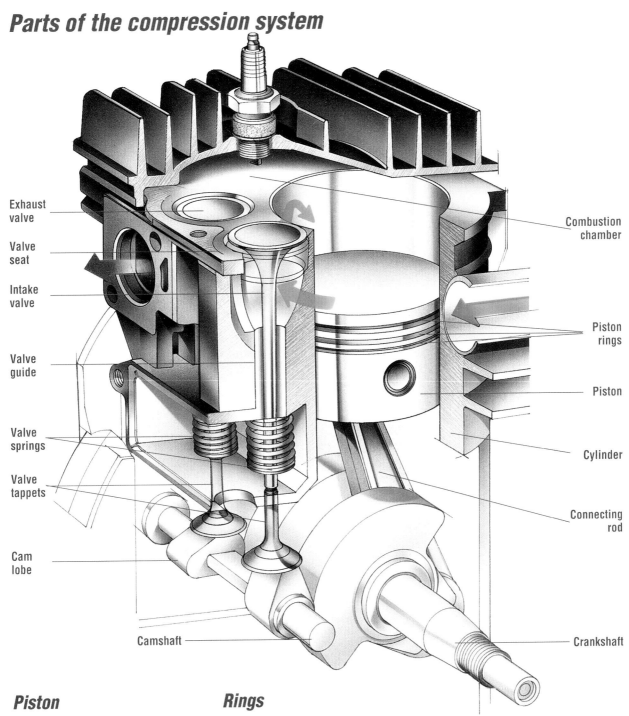

Exhaust valve

Valve seat

Intake valve

Valve guide

Valve springs

Valve tappets

Cam lobe

Camshaft

Combustion chamber

Piston rings

Piston

Cylinder

Connecting rod

Crankshaft

Piston

The **piston** rides through the **cylinder**, much as a plunger rides through the chamber in a hand-operated air pump. At the appropriate moment, the cylinder is sealed so that the air-fuel mixture is compressed as the piston moves toward the cylinder head. When the mixture is ignited, rapidly expanding gases force the piston back down through the cylinder.

Rings

The piston diameter is narrow enough to permit a thin space around it for a coating of oil. Flexible **piston rings**, installed in grooves in the piston, work in concert with the oil to create a seal between the piston and the cylinder wall. This ensures good compression.

As the piston is pushed down through the cylinder by expanding gases, a **connecting rod** transfers the force of those gases to the **flywheel**. It's the flywheel's momentum that perpetuates the engine's four-stroke cycle.

Compression problems

Too little or too much compression can damage pistons, rings, valves, **valve guides, valve seats** and the cylinder wall. If an exhaust valve leaks, exhaust can back up into the cylinder, causing premature wear. Too much compression can cause the air-fuel mixture to burn too fast, causing knocking or pinging. Excess compression can leave carbon deposits that further aggravate problems.

The four-stroke cycle

In most engines, including the one you'll find on your car, lawn mower, tractor, tiller, wood chipper or other outdoor power equipment, combustion occurs in a four-stroke cycle. The four-stroke cycle involves four distinct piston strokes (intake, compression, power and exhaust) that occur in succession. For each complete cycle, there are two complete rotations of the crankshaft.

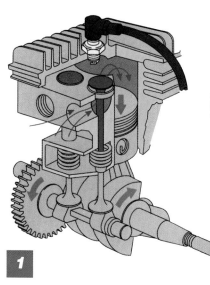

1

The Intake Stroke

During the intake stroke, a mixture of air and fuel is introduced to the combustion chamber. The intake valve is open and the piston moves from Top Dead Center (TDC) to Bottom Dead Center (BDC).

To understand what happens next, think of the suction produced like a syringe drawing liquid. This happens because as the plunger inside slides toward the handle, it creates a low-pressure area at the tip. A piston performs the identical task. As the piston moves toward BDC, it creates a low-pressure area in the cylinder and draws the air-fuel mixture through the intake valve. The mixture continues to flow, due to inertia, as the piston moves beyond BDC. Once the piston moves a few degrees beyond BDC, the intake valve closes, sealing the air-fuel mixture inside the cylinder.

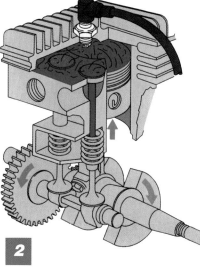

2

The Compression Stroke

Compression occurs as the piston travels toward TDC, squeezing the air-fuel mixture to a smaller volume. The air-fuel mixture is compressed for a more efficient burn and to allow more energy to be released faster when the mixture is ignited. Think about the warning label on pressurized spray cans: Keep contents away from fire. This is not only because the contents are flammable, but because pressurization makes them potentially explosive.

If an engine has to perform so much work just to bring the air-fuel mixture to the point of combustion, where does it find the ability to perform work? This ability derives from the fact that the energy required for compression—and stored in the flywheel—is still far less than the force produced during combustion. In a typical small engine, compression requires one-fourth the energy produced during combustion. The surplus drives the power stroke.

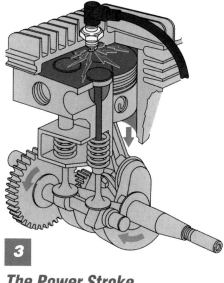

3

The Power Stroke

The engine's intake and exhaust valves are now closed. At approximately 20° before TDC, the spark plug initiates combustion, creating a flame that burns the compressed air-fuel mixture. The hot gases produced by combustion have no way to escape, so they push the piston away from the cylinder head. That motion is transferred through the connecting rod to apply torque to the crankshaft.

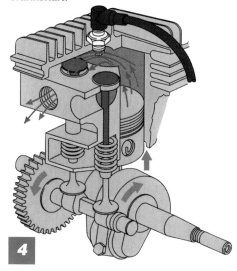

4

The Exhaust Stroke

As the piston reaches BDC during the power stroke, the power stroke is completed. The exhaust valve opens, allowing the piston to evacuate exhaust as it moves, once again, toward TDC. With the chamber cleared of exhaust, the piston reaches TDC. An entire cycle is complete.

Overhead valves (OHV) : the new standard

Locating the **valves** next to the piston is just one way to configure an engine. Engineers figured out long ago that they could gain a significant advantage in many higher-horsepower engines by installing the valves in the cylinder head so that they face the piston. Pivoting **rocker arms**—moved by **push rods**—open the valves.

One of the main advantages of overhead valve design is a more symmetrical combustion chamber, resulting in a more efficient burning of the air-fuel mixture. Briggs & Stratton is leading the way in the use of overhead valves in small engines. You may see the letters "OHV" imprinted on the shroud of your engine to indicate the use of overhead valves.

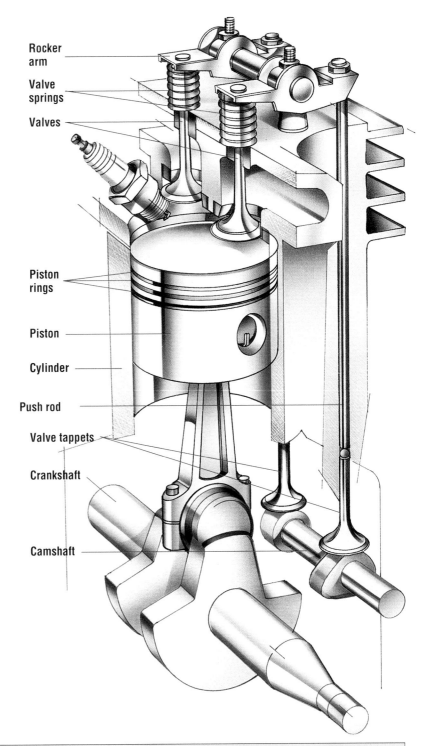

Rocker arm
Valve springs
Valves
Piston rings
Piston
Cylinder
Push rod
Valve tappets
Crankshaft
Camshaft

The two-stroke alternative

In a two-stroke engine, the piston acts as a valve, exposing the intake and exhaust ports at designated moments in the cycle. Two-stroke engines are still widely used for chain saws, leaf blowers and other hand-held equipment. They are also common for outboard motors and motocross motorcycles. They are no longer used on street bikes in many countries because of the two-stroke engine's higher emissions.

In the past, two-stroke engines were preferred for hand-held equipment because of their lightweight design. The same five events (intake, compression, combustion, power and exhaust) that occur in a four-stroke engine occur using fewer parts. However, the latest technology has reduced the weight of four-stroke engine components, creating the potential for inroads in the hand-held equipment industry.

FUEL SYSTEM

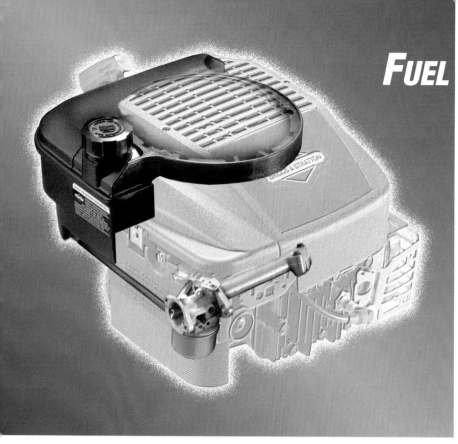

The most common repairs involve the fuel system, which includes the fuel tank, fuel filter, fuel line, fuel pump (on some models) and carburetor.

You may have heard people jokingly comment that the fuel in the tank is so low the engine is running "on vapors." Technically, they're right. Gasoline won't burn in its liquid state; it must be converted to a vapor first. The vapors that burn in your small engine are formed from a mixture of fuel (typically gasoline) and air. And you need the right amount of fuel and the right amount of air to maintain whatever engine speed you select. The best way to understand the fuel system is to begin at the tank.

From the fuel tank to the carburetor

Locate the **fuel tank** on your engine. If you have an older engine, it's probably made of steel or aluminum. Newer tanks are made of plastic and are built into the molded plastic shroud over the engine. Now, look for a **fuel line,** a hose connected to one side of the tank. The fuel line carries the fuel to the **carburetor,** a mixing chamber that contains a throttle and (if equipped) a choke, attached to the equipment controls.

On most engines, the force of gravity carries the fuel through the fuel line. However, if the fuel tank is mounted low on the engine, gravity may not do the trick. In this case, a **fuel pump** uses low pressure in the crankcase to pump fuel. The pump is located between the tank and the carburetor or in the carburetor itself.

Some engines eliminate the need for either a fuel line or pump by mounting the carburetor directly on the fuel tank and using a pick-up tube in the tank to draw fuel.

Parts of the Fuel System

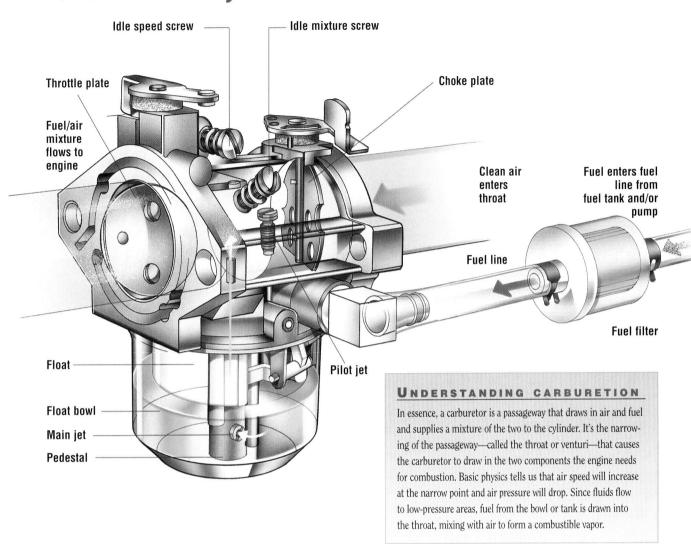

Idle speed screw

Idle mixture screw

Throttle plate

Fuel/air mixture flows to engine

Choke plate

Clean air enters throat

Fuel enters fuel line from fuel tank and/or pump

Fuel line

Fuel filter

Float

Float bowl

Main jet

Pedestal

Pilot jet

UNDERSTANDING CARBURETION

In essence, a carburetor is a passageway that draws in air and fuel and supplies a mixture of the two to the cylinder. It's the narrowing of the passageway—called the throat or venturi—that causes the carburetor to draw in the two components the engine needs for combustion. Basic physics tells us that air speed will increase at the narrow point and air pressure will drop. Since fluids flow to low-pressure areas, fuel from the bowl or tank is drawn into the throat, mixing with air to form a combustible vapor.

Into the carburetor

On most engines, fuel from the fuel line enters the carburetor's *fuel bowl,* a reservoir where a *float,* similar to the float ball in a toilet tank, regulates the fuel level. From there, a metering device called a *jet* lets fuel into the *emulsion tube* inside the *pedestal,* where fuel and air first mix. (Older models include an adjustable jet; newer models contain a fixed jet.) Fuel travels through the emulsion tube to the main passageway in the carburetor, called the *throat* or venturi, where further mixing occurs.

If your carburetor is a tank-mounted type, fuel from the tank may be supplied directly to the emulsion tube, without the need for a float.

The role of the throttle

At one end of the throat is a *throttle plate.* The throttle plate is connected to your equipment control lever (often referred to as the throttle) and opens or closes to increase or decrease engine speed. As the throttle plate opens, more air is drawn into the carburetor. Air flow, in turn, determines how much fuel is delivered for combustion (see "Understanding Carburetion," above).

Many carburetors have an *idle speed screw* to stop the throttle from closing too far at low speed, and an *idle mixture screw,* which increases or decreases air and fuel flow to prevent a stall.

Using the choke

A throttle works fine in warm weather. But when it's cold, fluids don't vaporize as easily. The engine may need extra fuel to start.

This is the role of the *choke plate* or *primer*. They compensate for the cold by increasing the fuel-to-air ratio. The choke is located in the throat between the air filter and the throttle plate. Closing the choke reduces air flow. Low pressure created inside the engine keeps the fuel flowing. The use of the choke "enriches the mixture." It's not an effective way to run an engine all the time, but it helps a cold engine start. Once the engine reaches its normal operating temperature range, you can open the choke to let in more air, for a cleaner, more efficient burn.

IGNITION SYSTEM

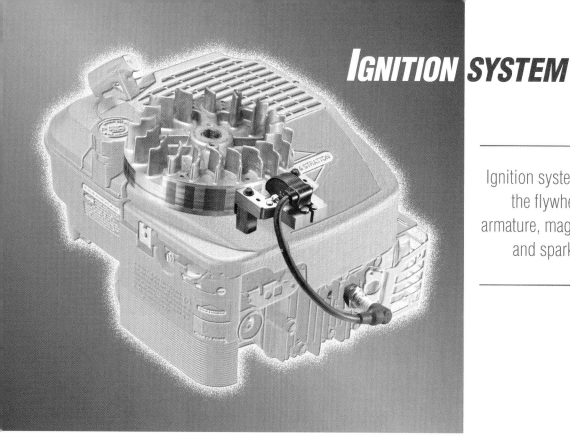

Ignition system parts include the flywheel, ignition armature, magnets, spark plug and spark plug lead.

*T*he ignition system is the starting system for your small engine. Whether you start the engine with a tug on the **rewind rope** or the turn of a key on an electric starter motor, you're relying on the ignition system to produce a spark inside the combustion chamber.

The ignition system includes **magnets** mounted in the surface of the **flywheel**, and an **ignition armature** mounted adjacent to the flywheel, containing copper wire windings. It also includes the **spark plug lead** (attached to the armature) and the **spark plug.**

When you pull on the rewind rope, you are turning the flywheel, a heavy metal wheel located under the blower housing. With each turn, the magnets mounted in the surface of the flywheel pass the ignition armature, inducing electrical flow that produces a high-voltage spark at the tip of the spark plug. The ignition system is coordinated with the tim-

ing of the piston and the motion of the valves so that the spark will ignite the air-fuel mixture in the combustion chamber just as the piston reaches the point of maximum compression in each engine cycle.

Once the engine is running, the flywheel's inertia keeps the crankshaft spinning until the piston's next power stroke, while the flywheel magnets induce voltage in the armature to keep the spark plug firing.

Solid-state ignition systems

It takes 10,000 to 20,000 volts of current to produce a spark at the tip of a spark plug. That's enough to give a person a powerful jolt. Today's ignition systems accomplish this using a tiny transistor in the ignition armature. Each time the magnets approach, the transistor establishes an electrical circuit, also called "closing" a circuit. The 2 to 3 amps of current produced are then converted to high-voltage current that travels through the spark plug lead to the spark plug.

Parts of the ignition system

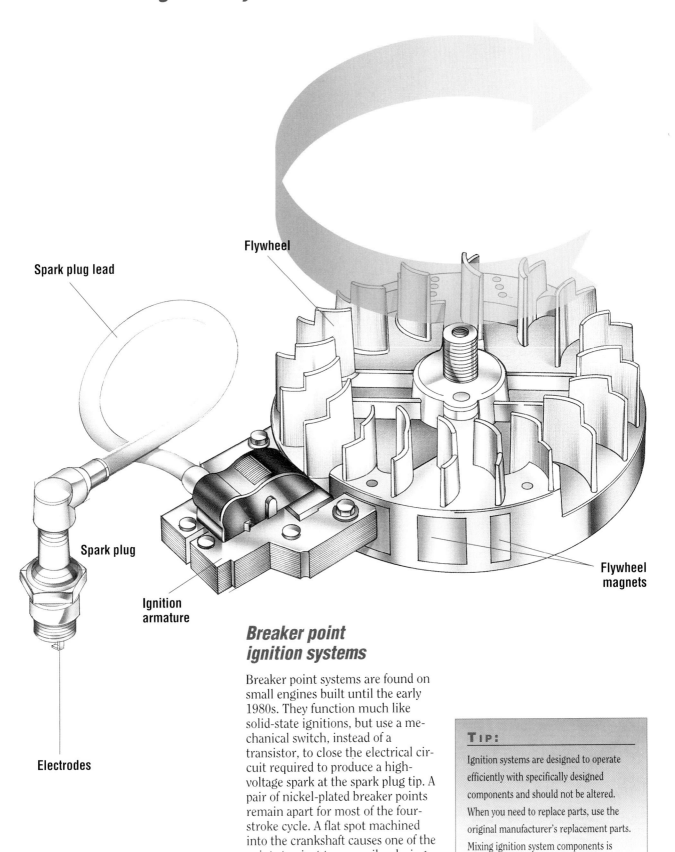

Spark plug lead

Flywheel

Spark plug

Ignition armature

Electrodes

Flywheel magnets

Breaker point ignition systems

Breaker point systems are found on small engines built until the early 1980s. They function much like solid-state ignitions, but use a mechanical switch, instead of a transistor, to close the electrical circuit required to produce a high-voltage spark at the spark plug tip. A pair of nickel-plated breaker points remain apart for most of the four-stroke cycle. A flat spot machined into the crankshaft causes one of the points to pivot temporarily, closing the gap between the two and closing a circuit.

> **TIP:**
>
> Ignition systems are designed to operate efficiently with specifically designed components and should not be altered. When you need to replace parts, use the original manufacturer's replacement parts. Mixing ignition system components is likely to cause engine malfunction.

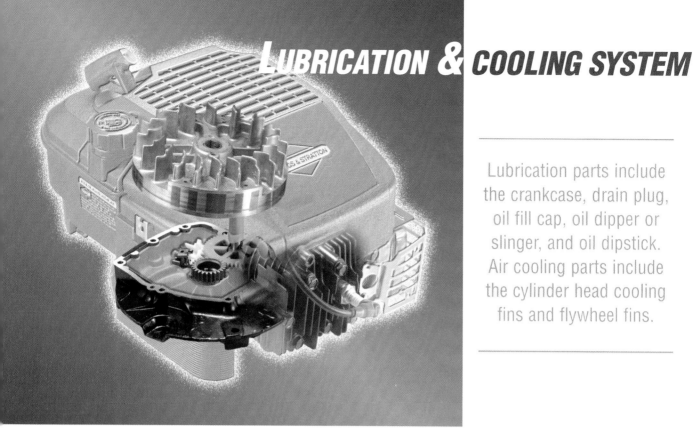

LUBRICATION & COOLING SYSTEM

Lubrication parts include the crankcase, drain plug, oil fill cap, oil dipper or slinger, and oil dipstick. Air cooling parts include the cylinder head cooling fins and flywheel fins.

Exhaust gases and radiant heat emitted from engine components carry off much of the heat produced by a small engine, but not enough to keep an engine running reliably. The lubrication and cooling system is designed to handle that task. As a lubricant, oil not only carries away heat, it reduces a major source of heat—friction between engine components. Air flow also serves a secondary function on some engines, triggering the **air vane** in a pneumatic governor (see "Governor System," pages 30 to 31).

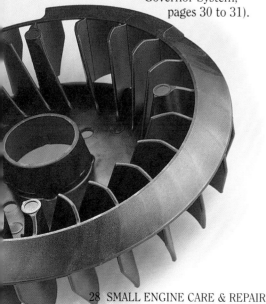

Reducing friction with oil

Viscosity is the most important quality of engine oil. It is a measure of an oil's ability to resist motion. This quality is critical to oil's performance, since moving parts constantly try to push oil, much as a plow pushes snow. Oil must resist this force so it can maintain a continuous film that keeps the parts themselves from touching.

While viscosity allows oil to cling to surfaces and resist the snow-plow effect, it also reduces the ability to flow at low temperatures or within tight clearances. A more viscous oil also takes longer to reach its optimal temperature.

Oil grades are generally a compromise that tries to anticipate typical operating conditions. A common recommendation for small engine oil is SAE (Society of Automotive Engineers) 30 four-cycle oil.

Some oils are altered to make them less viscous during the winter. These multi-viscosity oils have ratings such as SAE 10W-30. The 10W indicates a lower winter viscosity. At normal operating temperatures, the oil acts like SAE 30 oil. Always

follow the recommendation of your owner's manual when selecting the proper oil for your engine.

Getting oil to circulate

Most small engines rely on the splashing motion of a **dipper** or **slinger** in the **crankcase** to distribute oil. On a horizontal crankshaft engine, a dipper is attached to the connecting rod. It picks up oil in the oil reservoir located in the crankcase and spreads it across bearing surfaces as the piston travels through the cylinder.

A slinger is used on many vertical crankshaft engines. It consists of a spinning gear with **paddles** cast into the plastic **gear body**. Part of the slinger is submerged in the oil. As the crankshaft turns, the slinger disperses oil throughout the crankcase.

Keeping oil clean

Small engines designed for tractors and other heavy-duty equipment may include an **oil filter**. The pleated paper inside removes dirt, metal particles and other foreign matter that accumulates in the oil. If the becomes clogged, oil is rerouted through a spring-loaded **bypass valve** to ensure lubrication even when oil is very dirty. Even if your engine has an oil filter, you need to inspect the oil every time the engine is run to make sure the level is correct and the oil still has its clean amber color.

Cooling with air

An engine relies on air circulating around engine parts to maintain an acceptable engine temperature. **Fins** on the outside of the **cylinder block** and **cylinder head** improve the engine's cooling ability the way pipes do on a car radiator—by increasing the surface area that radiates heat and is exposed to cool air. Although air is not the most efficient way to transfer heat, it is plentiful and usually offers a substantial cooling effect.

A different set of fins—the **flywheel fins**—are also an important cooling feature; as they spin they distribute air to many engine parts. The **blower housing** and **air guides** route air to the flywheel fins. On some models, a **rotating screen** over the flywheel prevents grass and other debris from clogging the flywheel fins. The screen blocks debris from entering or cuts it into smaller, less harmful particles.

Additional cooling components

Some engines require additional air cooling and contain a cooling **air plenum,** a duct that provides a separate means for outside air to enter the engine. Some contain an **air discharge** that directs hot air away from the engine.

USING MULTI-VISCOSITY OIL

Multi-viscosity oil, such as SAE 10W-30, is designed to work well in cold weather. It's not the best choice if you typically operate your equipment at or above 40°F. In warm weather, multi-viscosity oil is likely to cause premature carbon build-up and loss of engine power.

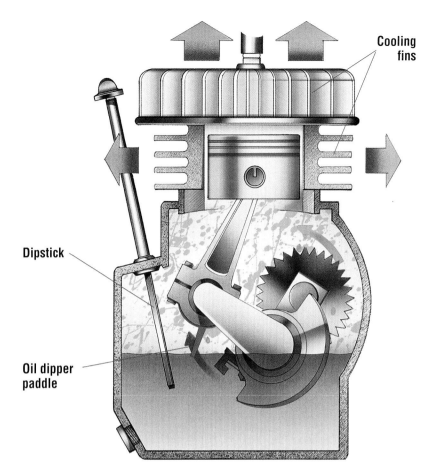

Cooling fins

Dipstick

Oil dipper paddle

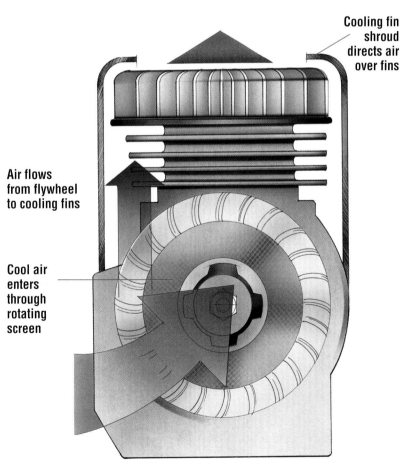

Cooling fin shroud directs air over fins

Air flows from flywheel to cooling fins

Cool air enters through rotating screen

GOVERNOR SYSTEM

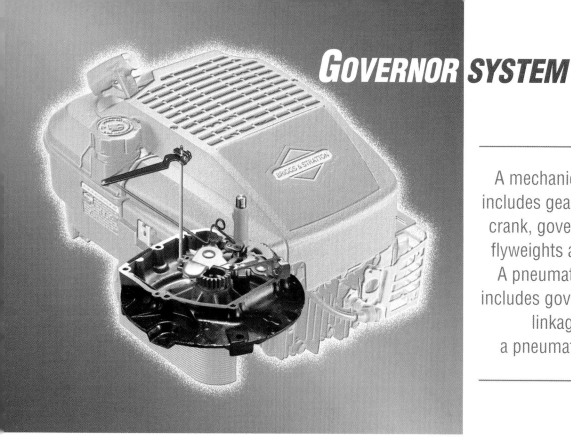

A mechanical governor includes gears, a governor crank, governor springs, flyweights and linkages. A pneumatic governor includes governor springs, linkages and a pneumatic air vane.

The governor system is like a cruise control system. It keeps the engine running at the speed you select, regardless of changes in the load. You can think of the load as the amount of work the engine must perform: for a mower, the height of the grass; for a tiller, the depth of the tines; for a chipper, the thickness of the branches.

Without a governor, you would need to adjust the throttle manually each time your lawn mower ran across a dense patch of grass. A governor does the job for you by detecting changes in the load and adjusting the throttle to compensate.

How a governor functions

The governor system behaves like an unending tug of war between one or two *governor springs,* which pull the throttle toward the open position, and a spinning crankshaft, which tries to close the throttle. When the load on the engine increases—a typical example is when you move your running lawn mower from the driveway to the grass—crankshaft revolutions drop. But the governor spring is still tugging, causing the throttle plate to open.

In response, a larger volume of air-fuel mixture enters the carburetor, increasing engine speed to compensate for the increased load. The crankshaft speeds up, and the tug of war resumes, until a new equilibrium is achieved.

With each change in load, the tension between the governor spring and the load brings about a new equilibrium, known as the engine's governed speed.

Neither side wins until the engine is shut off. At that point, without the crankshaft spinning, the governor spring pulls the throttle to the wide-open position.

Two types of governor are common on small engines—mechanical and pneumatic.

Mechanical governor

A mechanical governor uses *gears* and *flyweights* inside the crankcase as a speed-sensing device that detects changes in the load and adjusts the throttle accordingly. If you're operating your small engine under a light load, the carburetor needs to deliver a relatively small amount of air-fuel mixture to the combustion chamber. As the crankshaft spins, centrifugal force causes the flyweights to open. As they open, they apply pressure to the *governor cup* and *governor crank,* which are linked to the throttle. The throttle is pulled toward the closed position.

As the load on the crankshaft increases, the flyweights spin more slowly. The reduced centrifugal force on the flyweights results in less pull on the throttle toward the closed position. But since the governor spring tension remains, the throttle reopens until the desired governed speed is achieved.

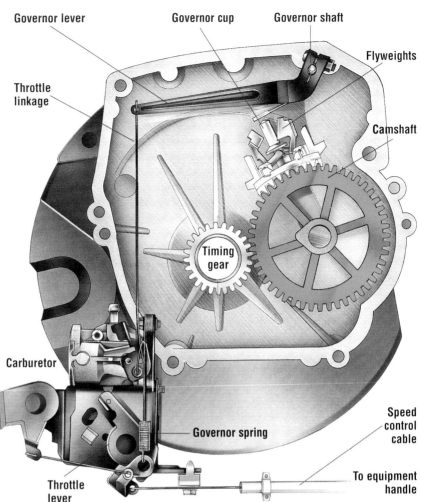

Governor lever · Governor cup · Governor shaft · Flyweights · Camshaft · Throttle linkage · Timing gear · Carburetor · Governor spring · Speed control cable · Engine speed control · Throttle lever · To equipment handle

Pneumatic governor

A pneumatic governor uses a movable *air vane,* made of metal or plastic, as a speed-sensing device by registering the change in air pressure around the spinning flywheel. The pneumatic governor design is simpler and parts are easier to access. It is also a slightly less reliable design, since small particles of debris can interfere with the pneumatic governor's operation.

The pneumatic governor also relies on one or two springs to pull the throttle toward the open position. As the load lessens and engine speed increases, air blown by the flywheel also begins to increase, causing the governor blade to pull the throttle plate toward the closed position in its effort to maintain a steady engine speed.

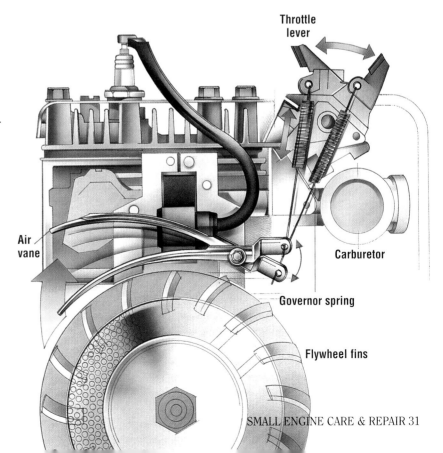

Throttle lever · Air vane · Carburetor · Governor spring · Flywheel fins

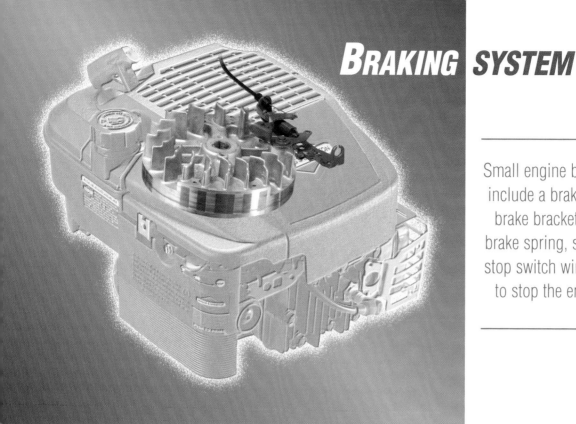

BRAKING SYSTEM

Small engine braking systems include a brake band or pad, brake bracket, brake cover, brake spring, stop switch and stop switch wire, all designed to stop the engine quickly.

In the old days, you could leave your lawn mower or tractor idling while you stepped into the garage for a rake. Today's small engine contains an automatic shut-off system designed to protect you and others in the area by stopping the engine any time you let go of the controls or climb off of the equipment.

Many small engines contain a brake that applies pressure to the smooth surface on the *flywheel.* The brake's surface area varies in size, depending on the equipment. Some models use a ***brake pad.*** Others use a ***brake band,*** applied to a larger area on the flywheel's surface. Both are highly effective when properly maintained.

Most engines contain one or more ***stop switches*** wired between the engine's ignition system and engine and equipment components. You can trigger the switch by releasing the ***brake bail*** or removing the grass discharge unit on a lawn mower or by standing up from the seat of a lawn tractor, triggering a switch under the seat.

The switch cuts power to the engine by grounding one of the copper windings in the ignition armature (see "Ignition System," pages 26 to 27). When the brake bail is released, a wire attached to the armature is grounded against a metal engine part, stopping the engine. If the engine is equipped with a brake, the brake pad or band simultaneously applies pressure to the flywheel. When properly maintained, the two components of the braking system stop the engine within three seconds.

Parts of the braking system

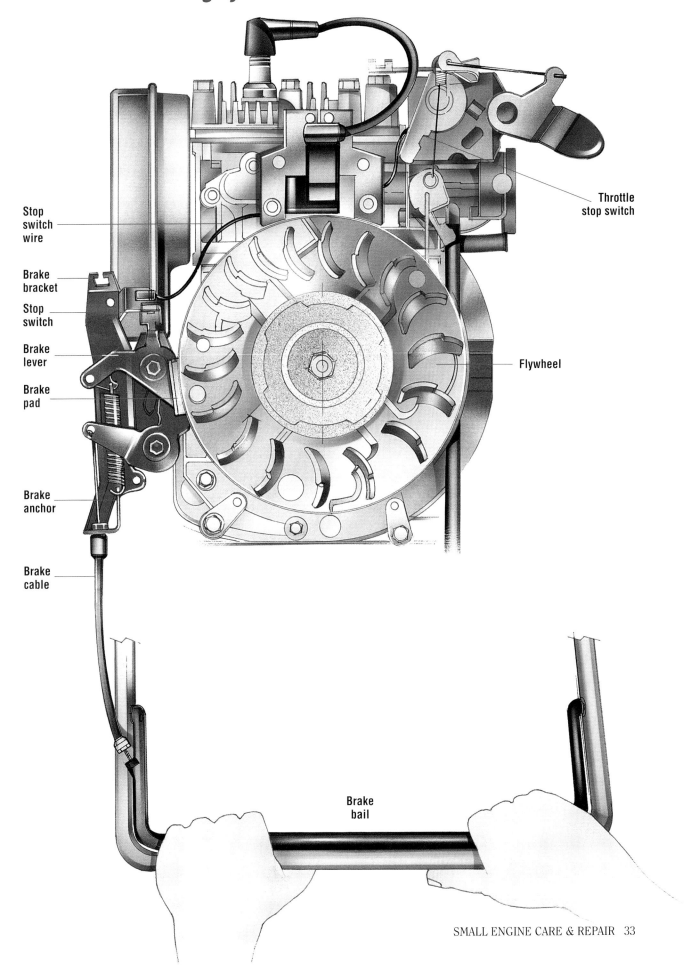

Stop switch wire

Brake bracket

Stop switch

Brake lever

Brake pad

Brake anchor

Brake cable

Throttle stop switch

Flywheel

Brake bail

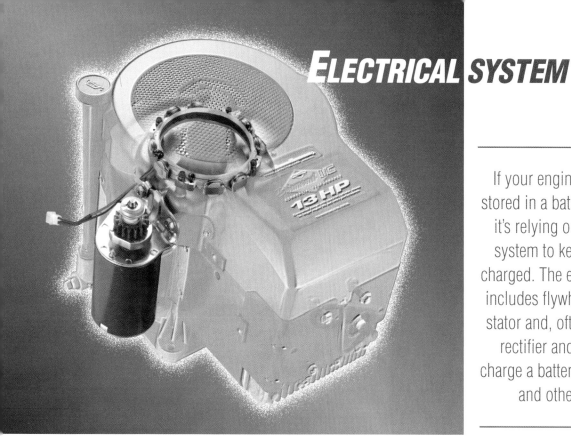

ELECTRICAL SYSTEM

If your engine uses energy stored in a battery for starting, it's relying on an electrical system to keep the battery charged. The electrical system includes flywheel magnets, a stator and, often, a regulator, rectifier and capacitor to charge a battery and run lights and other devices.

A small engine electrical system typically consists of an *alternator, rectifier, regulator* and 12-volt *battery.* The alternator itself consists of an assembly of one or more copper windings—collectively known as the *stator*—and a set of *magnets.* Like the ignition system, the alternator creates a moving magnetic field to induce current.

Most stators consist of a band of non-adjustable windings mounted under the flywheel and a set of magnets cemented to the inside surface of the flywheel. On some engines, the stator consists of an adjustable armature mounted outside the flywheel that relies on the same magnets as the ignition armature to charge the battery. The result is longer periods of time between surges of voltage and current. Limited amounts of DC voltage and current are produced, and a *capacitor* is used to handle fluctuations in the voltage output.

Parts of the electrical system

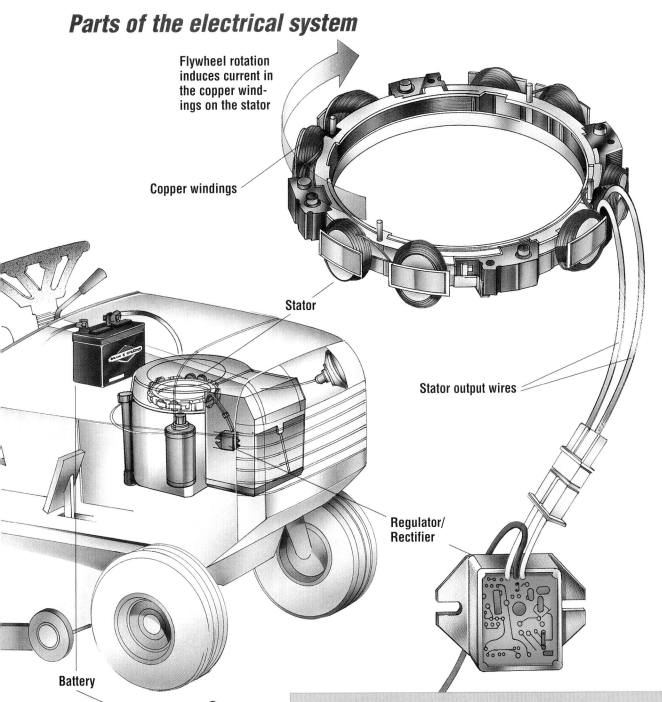

Flywheel rotation induces current in the copper windings on the stator

Copper windings

Stator

Stator output wires

Regulator/Rectifier

Battery

Alternating current vs. direct current

An electrical system can be set up to produce either alternating current (AC) or direct current (DC). If your equipment runs lights and no battery or other electrical devices, the alternator operates much like the generator on a bicycle wheel, keeping the lights running with AC as long as the bike wheel (or the engine crankshaft) is spinning.

If your equipment includes a battery and various electrical devices, a rectifier is attached to the alternator to convert AC power to DC so it can be stored in the battery. DC power can run lights even when the engine is off, as well as a starter motor, electric cutting blade clutch, winch and other devices. Some engines supply AC for lights and DC for other devices.

Engines that operate at high speeds also require a regulator or a combined regulator/rectifier to maintain a steady voltage output.

MAINTENANCE

March Is Mower Tune-Up Month!

Why Tune Up?

A simple and inexpensive tune-up provides many benefits to you and the environment, including:

- Extending the life of your equipment and saving money. Regular tune-ups keep equipment running in tip-top shape, thus extending the life of the engine and the mower. This reduces repair costs and minimizes the likelihood of prematurely replacing individual parts or even the entire engine. It is also a great way to protect your warranty coverage — and your investment.
- Improving the startability of your engine.
- Reducing fuel consumption up to 30 percent, which conserves natural resources.
- Reducing emissions up to 50 percent, which protects the environment.
- Restoring your horsepower by 7.5 percent. A well-tuned engine runs at full strength to get the job done quickly and easily.

When it comes to keeping your mower running efficiently, the best thing for it is an annual tune-up. And it's one of the best things you can do for the environment, too.

To bring attention to the benefits of annual tune-ups, Briggs & Stratton and the National Wildlife Federation have teamed up for the annual campaign, March Is Mower Tune-Up Month. This national campaign reminds mower owners that a properly tuned mower will not only perform better, but be better for the environment.

The benefits of a simple, inexpensive tune-up include reducing emissions by as much as 50 percent, lowering fuel consumption by up to 30 percent, and restoring horsepower up to 7.5 percent. Briggs & Stratton and the National Wildlife Federation encourage mower users everywhere to make Mower Tune-Up Month their first step toward performing annual tune-ups — for the good of your investment *and* the environment.

How to Tune Up...

There are two easy ways to keep your machine tuned up: Do it yourself in about 30 minutes or take your machine to a Briggs & Stratton service dealer.

- **For do-it-yourselfers**, Briggs & Stratton offers easy-to-use maintenance kits, complete with oil, air filter, spark plug and fuel stabilizer. Maintenance kits are available at Briggs & Stratton dealers and select retailers.
- **For a professional tune-up**, you can take your mower to one of the 30,000 Briggs & Stratton dealers worldwide. Some dealers even offer pickup and delivery or at-home service. Be sure to ask.

For more information on National Mower Tune-Up Month, visit www.tuneupmonth.com. The site provides helpful tips on selecting the right maintenance kit, locating retailers and dealers who sell the kits and simple how-to instructions for performing a tune-up.

For the do-it-yourselfer, Briggs & Stratton offers an easy-to-use maintenance kit, complete with all the essential tune-up elements: See page 39 for choosing the right maintenance kit.

A Quick & Easy Tune-Up Process

Performing your own tune-up is a simple 4-step process. You'll find everything you need for a tune-up plus easy-to-follow instructions in your maintenance kit.

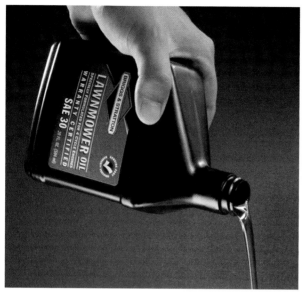

Changing Oil

Changing the oil keeps the engine properly lubricated and ensures clean oil is continuously distributed to critical engine components, reducing friction. Less friction results in less wear and tear on engine components.

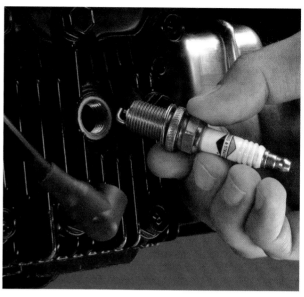

Spark Plug

An eroded or fouled spark plug provides an inconsistent spark. Replacing the spark plug in spring ensures a consistent spark, making starting more reliable and improving fuel economy.

Air Filter

Changing the air filter prevents clogging. A clogged air filter reduces the air/fuel ratio, resulting in higher fuel consumption. The lower air/fuel ratio also leads to excess or unburned gasoline, resulting in the release of extra hydrocarbons. Hydrocarbons form ground-level ozone, a major component of smog.

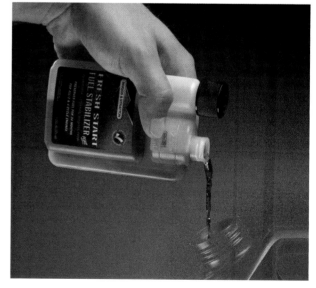

Fuel Stabilizer

Fuel stabilizer improves starting by preventing idle gasoline from degrading to the point where it is no longer combustible.

MAINTENANCE KITS

Selecting the Right Maintenance Kit

Our maintenance kits have everything you need to perform your own maintenance on your Briggs & Stratton engine. Performing a tune-up is a simple, 4-step process, and we'll show you how!

The Genuine Briggs & Stratton Maintenance Kits Include:

- replacement air filter
- oil
- replacement spark plug
- Fuel Stabilizer Plus
- detailed, easy-to-follow instructions that take you through the simple maintenance process!
- oil filter and fuel filter if applicable

Selecting and Purchasing Your Maintenance Kit

Find your engine model number or engine name and horsepower and look for your correct maintenance kit at www.tuneupmonth.com. Our search engine will help you find the right maintenance kit for your product. You can download the instructions for your maintenance kit, so you can see how easy it is to perform your tune-up! We even link you to where you can buy online or where you can find a local store.

Maintenance Reminder Email Service

The best time to tune up your mower for the season ahead is in early spring before you start mowing.

Want to be reminded of when to perform other annual maintenance on ALL your power equipment? Be sure to sign up for our FREE Maintenance Reminder Email service at www.tuneupmonth.com.

You can also view and print our Maintenance Schedule-at-a-Glance to plan ahead for the rest of the season.

TOOLS

Maintenance Minder and Maintenance Mate

Automobiles have maintenance reminders; why shouldn't your power equipment have them too? Briggs & Stratton's new Maintenance Minder™ (Hour Meter) indicates how many hours your machine has been used, then flashes when maintenance should be performed. It's easy to install and has a 3-year battery as well as a maintenance schedule sticker so you can see what maintenance needs to be done.

Maintenance Minder™
(Hour Meter) – Part No. 5081D
Display flashes every 25 hours of run time. For 2- and 4-cycle engines.

To complement the Briggs & Stratton Maintenance Kits, we now offer the Maintenance Mate™. It's a handy tool set to help you change your Briggs & Stratton parts on your outdoor power equipment. The tool kit includes:

- 17/32" Oil Drain Socket
- 7/16" Oil Drain Socket
- 13/16" Spark Plug Socket
- 5/18" Spark Plug Socket
- Air Cleaner Screwdriver

Maintenance Mate™
Part No. 5082D
Tools to use for preventative maintenance on most Briggs & Stratton engines.

Your Resource on the Web

Visit our Web site at **www.BriggsandStratton.com** to find everything you need to know about all your Briggs & Stratton power equipment, including lawnmowers, pressure washers and generators.

For more information on National Mower Tune-Up Month, visit **www.tuneupmonth.com**. There you'll find helpful tips on selecting the right maintenance kit, locat-

ing retailers and dealers who sell the kits, and simple how-to instructions for performing a tune-up.

And what's your best prescription for a healthy lawn? Find out from **www.yarddoctor.com**. There you'll get the Yarddoctor's expert advice on lawn care, from proper preparation to healthy maintenance.

MAINTENANCE

Regular maintenance schedule

You can avoid many small engine problems and save money on parts and repairs if you follow a regular maintenance schedule. Make good maintenance a habit when your engine is new, and always consult your owner's manual for special guidelines for your make and model. Service the engine more frequently if you use it heavily or under dusty or dirty conditions.

After the first five hours of use:

- Change the oil and filter (pages 46 to 49).

After each use:

- Check the oil (pages 46 to 49).
- Remove debris around the muffler (pages 66 to 69).

Every 25 hours or every season:

- Change the oil if operating under heavy load or in hot weather (pages 46 to 49).
- Service the air cleaner assembly (pages 52 to 55).
- Clean the fuel tank and line (pages 70 to 71).
- Clean the carburetor float bowl, if equipped (pages 91 to 95).
- Inspect the rewind rope for wear (pages 86 to 87).
- Clean the cooling fins on the engine block (pages 66 to 69).
- Remove debris from the blower housing (pages 66 to 69).
- Check engine compression (pages 56 to 57).
- Inspect governor springs and linkages (pages 81 to 85).
- Inspect ignition armature and wires (pages 100 to 103).
- Inspect the muffler (pages 62 to 65).
- Check the valve tappet clearances (page 117).
- Replace the spark plug (pages 50 to 51).
- Adjust the carburetor (pages 76 to 79).
- Check the engine mounting bolts/nuts (pages 56 to 57).

Every 100 hours or every season:

- Clean the cooling system (pages 66 to 69).*
- Change the oil filter, if equipped (pages 46 to 49).
- Decarbonize the cylinder head (pages 108 to 111).

Clean more often if the engine operates under dusty conditions or in tall, dry grass.

End-of-season maintenance

Engines are built to run. But many small engines are only used seasonally and sit idle for long periods. Long-term storage can aggravate overlooked problems, and other problems can develop. For example, unstabilized gas left in an engine can gum up a carburetor, unlubricated engine parts can corrode, and moisture can accumulate in the ignition system. With proper storage preparation, you can avoid most such problems. If you plan to store your engine for more than 30 days:

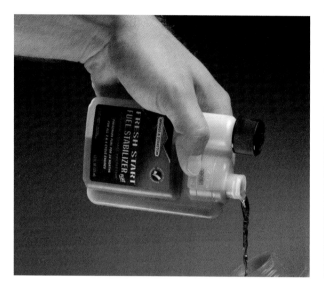

Drain the gasoline

Gasoline that's allowed to stand for over a month may form a varnish on the inside of the fuel tank, carburetor and other fuel system components. Draining the gasoline reduces varnish problems. Drain the carburetor float bowl (if equipped) as well. The Environmental Protection Agency recommends adding the drained gasoline to your car's gas tank, provided your car tank is fairly full. Once diluted, old gasoline will not harm your car engine. Another way to protect against the varnishing effects of old fuel is to add a gasoline stabilizer such as Briggs & Stratton Gasoline Additive, to your fuel, before storage (pages 70 to 71).

Change the oil

Changing the oil will prevent particles of dirt in the oil from adhering to engine parts (pages 46 to 49).

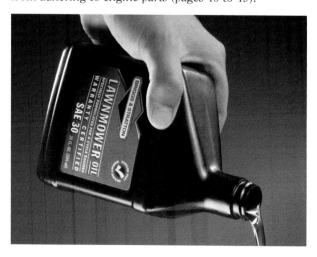

Seal the fuel cap

Your small engine emits small amounts of fuel vapor into the air—even when it's not running. To reduce emissions during storage, cover the vented fuel cap with aluminum foil and secure it with an elastic band (pages 70 to 71).

Lubricate internal parts

Injecting oil through the spark plug hole is an easy way to lubricate the cylinder. Just squirt about ½ oz. of fogging oil into the spark plug hole. Then, spread it throughout the cylinder by reattaching the spark plug and slowly pulling the rewind.

Inspect the spark plug

Clean and regap the spark plug or replace it, as necessary (pages 50 to 51).

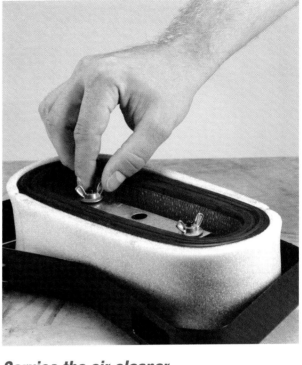

Service the air cleaner

This step can extend the life of the air cleaner and improve engine performance next season (pages 52 to 55).

Seal the combustion chamber

You can prevent varnish formation in the combustion chamber during storage by placing the piston at top dead center (TDC), the point at which both valves are closed. This keeps out stale fuel and debris. Just pull the rewind rope slowly. When you feel increased tension on the rope (due to the compression of air in the chamber), the piston is at TDC (pages 20 to 23).

Remove dirt and debris

Debris tends to accumulate in the cylinder head fins, under the blower housing and around the muffler. This debris can fall into the engine. Remove it now to ensure good performance next season. Then, cover the engine with a sheet of plastic and store in a dry place (pages 66 to 69).

CHECKING & CHANGING OIL

Tools & materials:
Socket wrench set, box
wrench or adjustable
wrench, screwdriver
or hex key,
oil filter or pipe wrench
(for models with filters),
oil drain pan, funnel.

Time required:
30 minutes.

When you pour fresh oil into the crankcase, it's a golden or amber color. Gradually, the heat, dirt particles and agitated air in the crankcase cause the oil to darken. Dark oil is not only dirty; it has also lost much of its ability to coat and protect engine components.

Manufacturers recommend changing the oil in your small engine after every 25 hours of operation. For a new engine, you'll also need to change the oil after the first five hours of operation. New engines require this extra step to flush out small particles that accumulate naturally during the break-in period.

Hours of use are just one factor in determining how often the oil should be changed; the amount of wear and tear is equally important. Just like the oil in a vehicle operated in extremely dirty or dusty conditions or at high speeds, the oil in a lawn mower or other small engine breaks down faster under tough conditions, such as wet grass, heavy dust, high temperatures and rough or hilly terrain.

Avoid overfilling your crankcase. Too much oil can cause the same type of engine damage as not having enough. Air bubbles form in the oil, reducing overall lubrication. The resulting friction and metal-to-metal contact can cause premature part failure. Excess oil can also burn in the cylinder, producing smoke and leaving carbon deposits.

This section covers procedures for checking and changing oil and oil filters, and offers tips on avoiding spills and choosing the right oil and other products for your engine.

Checking the oil

Make it a habit to check the oil level and appearance each time you're about to start a small engine. Checking the oil while the engine is cold and most of the oil is in the crankcase yields the most accurate reading. You won't need to change or add oil every time. But you'll ensure a better-running engine and avoid problems down the road if you keep the crankcase full and change the oil on schedule and any time the oil loses its amber hue.

1. Start by locating the oil fill cap on the crankcase (photo A). Fill cap locations vary, depending on the make and model of your engine. On newer models, look for an oil can symbol or the word "oil" or "fill" stamped on the plug. On small tractors, you may have to lift the hood to locate this cap.

Some engines contain either an extended oil fill tube or a standard fill hole with a dipstick for inspection. Others require you to remove the fill cap to check that the oil is at the fill line or the top of the fill hole.

2. To prevent dirt and debris from falling into the crankcase, wipe the area around the cap with a clean cloth before removing the cap. If there is no dipstick, dab the oil with a clean tip of the cloth to inspect the oil (photo B).

3. If the engine includes a dipstick cap, remove the dipstick and wipe it with a clean cloth. To ensure an accurate reading, reinsert the dipstick completely. Then, remove it again and check the oil level. If the dipstick cap is a screw-in type, ensure an accurate reading by screwing it in all the way before removing it a second time to check the level. The oil mark on the dipstick should be between the lines shown on the dipstick (photo C). It should never be above the FULL line or below the ADD line.

Synthetic Oil

Uniquely blended for use in all engines, this all-season oil provides the extra protection you need in the most severe operating conditions. It exhibits excellent cold-weather flow characteristics that minimize engine wear and provide easier cold starting.

A

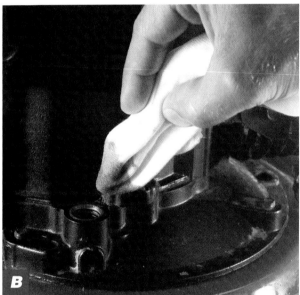

B

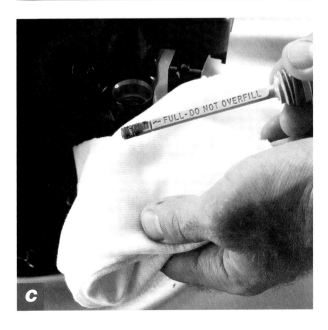

C

Changing the oil

Once you decide the oil needs changing, check your owner's manual to determine the type of oil, and make sure you have enough on hand. Then, run the engine for several minutes. Draining the oil while it's warm will carry off many floating particles that would otherwise settle in the engine.

1. Stop the engine, disconnect the spark plug lead and secure it away from the spark plug. Then, locate the oil drain plug. On mowers, the plug is typically below the deck and may be obscured by a layer of grass and debris.

2. Wipe the area with a rag to prevent debris from falling into the crankcase when you open the drain plug. Tilt the mower deck and position some newspaper and an oil pan or jug beneath the mower. Use a socket wrench to turn the plug counterclockwise, allowing the old oil to drain (photo A). If the plug also serves as a fill cap, it may have two prongs so you can loosen it by hand or use a screwdriver or hex key for additional torque. Replace the drain plug by twisting clockwise and tightening with a box wrench or adjustable wrench.

3. If your engine has a filter, replace it at least once a season, more often under heavy use (see "Regular Maintenance," page 43). Replace the filter by twisting counter-clockwise on the body, using a filter wrench or pipe wrench.

4. Lightly oil the filter gasket with clean engine oil. Install a new filter rated for your engine. Screw in the filter by hand until the gasket contacts the filter adapter (photo B). Tighten the filter an additional ½ to ¾ turn.

5. Add the appropriate quantity of oil (see your owner's manual). Then, run the engine at idle and check for leaks.

6. After an oil change, dispose of oil and soiled rags in accordance with local environmental statutes (photo C). In many areas, oil can be left at curbside with other recyclables, provided it is sealed in a recyclable container. Check the regulations in your area.

Choose the Proper Oil

(A) Snow Blower Oil – The 32 oz. bottle of SAE 5W30 oil has been specially formulated and approved for winter use in all air-cooled 4-cycle engines.

(B) 100% Synthetic Oil – Uniquely blended for use in all engines, this all-season oil provides the extra protection you need in the most severe operating conditions. It exhibits excellent cold-weather flow characteristics that minimize engine wear and provide easier cold starting.

(C) 2-Cycle Ashless Oil – A premium-quality ashless oil with gas stabilizer for use in air-cooled 2-cycle engines.

Ashless-oil formulation leaves no residue and prevents plug fouling and engine deposits.

Pre-diluted to mix quickly with leaded or unleaded gasoline and may be used in oil-injected systems.

(D) Marine/Outboard Oil – Specially formulated for 4-cycle engines in warm weather between 40 degrees and 100 degrees.

(E) Lawnmower Oil – Briggs & Stratton lawnmower oil is formulated to meet the unique demands created by air-cooled 4-cycle engines. Tested and approved by Briggs & Stratton engineers. Warranty certified and recommended in all Briggs & Stratton manuals. A high-quality detergent oil classified SG/CD by the API. Conveniently sized for today's engines.

TIP:

An oil evacuation pump is a clean and easy way to remove oil from your crankcase. The Briggs & Stratton pump (Part number 5056) attaches to the end of an electric drill. With one end of the attached hose, warm oil is pumped from the crankcase. The other end is inserted in a jug to drain the oil. NOTE: Never use the pump to evacuate gasoline or other fuel. Fuel vapors can easily ignite and erupt into flames in the presence of a spark from the drill.

SERVICING SPARK PLUGS

Tools & materials:
Spark tester, spark plug socket (sizes vary), socket wrench, wire brush, plug/point cleaner, spark plug gauge.

Time required:
15 minutes.

*T*he electrodes on a spark plug must be clean and sharp to produce the powerful spark required for ignition. The more worn or dirty a spark plug, the more voltage—and the greater the tug on the rewind—required to produce an adequate spark.

If you haven't tuned your engine recently and have to tug repeatedly on the rewind to start the engine, a damaged spark plug may be the culprit. Inconsistent firing, known as spark "miss," can result in sluggish engine operation and poor acceleration. A damaged spark plug may also cause excessive fuel consumption, deposits on the cylinder head and oil dilution.

Luckily, a spark plug is one of the easiest engine components to repair and an inexpensive one to replace. And your standard socket set may already include the most important tool—a spark plug socket.

This section covers the essentials of spark plug inspection and replacement. It shows you how to use a spark tester and how to adjust and clean a spark plug that is worn but still serviceable. Just remember, you can't go wrong by replacing it.

Cleaning and inspecting a spark plug

1. Disconnect the spark plug lead. Then, clean the area around the spark plug to avoid getting debris in the combustion chamber when you remove the plug.

2. Remove the spark plug using a spark plug socket.

3. Clean light deposits from the plug with a wire brush and spray-on plug cleaner. Then, use a sturdy knife if necessary to scrape off tough deposits. NOTE: Never clean a spark plug with a shot blaster or abrasives.

4. Inspect the spark plug for very stubborn deposits, or for cracked porcelain or electrodes that have been burned away. If any of these conditions exists, replace the spark plug.

5. Use a spark plug gauge to measure the gap between the two electrodes (one straight, one curved) at the tip of your spark plug (photo A). Many small engines require a .030" gap. Check the specifications for your model with your power equipment dealer. If necessary, use a spark plug gauge to adjust the gap by gently bending the curved electrode. When the gap is correct, the gauge will drag slightly as you pull it through the gap.

6. Reinstall the plug, taking care not to overtighten. Then, attach the spark plug lead.

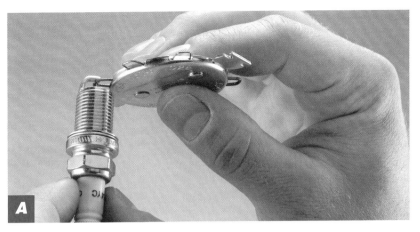

Checking ignition with a spark tester

A spark tester offers an inexpensive, easy way to diagnose ignition problems (see "Checking for Spark Miss").

If you find a problem, remove and inspect the spark plug. Replace the spark plug if you find evidence of wear or burning at the spark plug tip. Spark plugs are inexpensive and a new one may solve the problem.

1. Connect the spark plug lead to the long terminal of your tester and ground the tester to the engine with the tester's alligator clip (photo B).

2. Use the rewind or electric starter to crank the engine, and look for a spark in the tester's window.

3. If you see a spark jump the gap in the tester, the ignition is functioning. The absence of a visible spark indicates a problem in the ignition system.

Checking for spark miss

A spark plug that is fouled or improperly gapped may not allow sparks to jump the gap between electrodes consistently. The spark plug will fire erratically or may occasionally fail to spark. Test for this problem—known as spark "miss"—if your engine stumbles, with a noticeable decrease in engine sound. Spark miss can also cause the engine to emit black smoke or a popping sound, as unburned fuel exits with the exhaust and ignites inside the muffler.

1. With the spark plug screwed into the cylinder head, attach the spark plug lead to the long terminal of the spark tester. Attach the tester's alligator clip to the spark plug (photo C).

2. Start the engine and watch the tester's spark gap. You'll recognize spark miss by the uneven timing of the sparks in the tester.

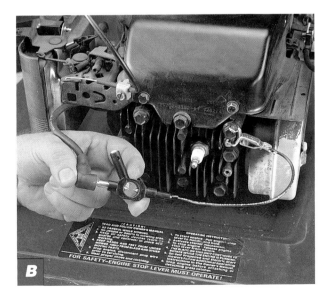

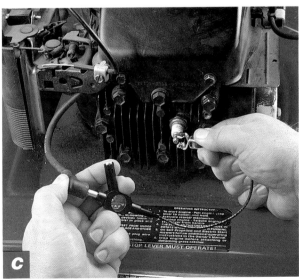

SERVICING AIR CLEANERS

Tools & materials:
Engine oil, screwdrivers, liquid detergent.

Time required:
30 minutes.

A properly maintained air cleaner is your engine's first line of defense against the destructive effects of dirt. When the air cleaner is in good condition, it keeps airborne dirt particles from entering through the carburetor. If the air cleaner is not maintained, dirt and dust will gradually make their way into the engine. And don't underestimate dirt's potential to cause damage. It can lead to a sharp drop in engine power, or—worse—cause premature wear of

critical engine components.

Many types of air cleaners are used in small engines. Most contain a foam or pleated-paper element.

Dual-element air cleaners contain a pleated-paper element with a foam pre-cleaner, offering two layers of protection. Discard the paper element when you can no longer remove dirt from the pleats by tapping the element on a hard, dry surface.

Single-element air cleaners should be replaced every 25 hours (or once a season). In a dual-element system, the pre-cleaner should be replaced every 25 hours. Refer to the photo (opposite) to identify the air cleaner on your engine.

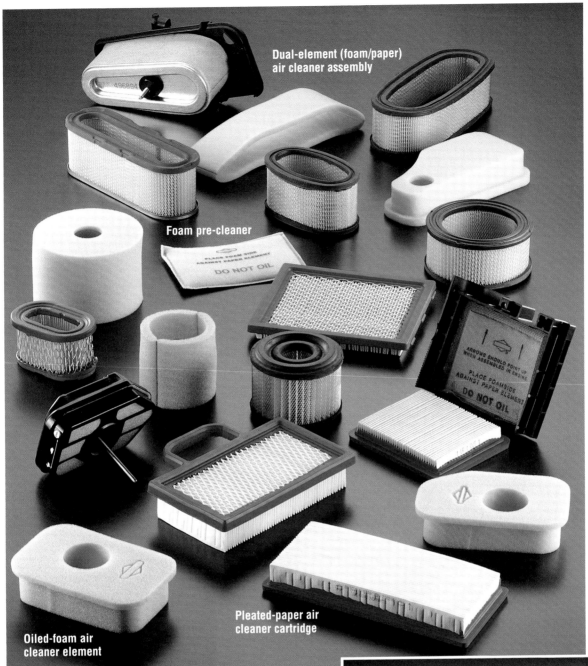

Dual-element (foam/paper) air cleaner assembly

Foam pre-cleaner

Pleated-paper air cleaner cartridge

Oiled-foam air cleaner element

Extended Life air filters

There are a variety of air cleaner designs. Some contain an oiled-foam element, others a pleated-paper cartridge. Newer engines often contain a combination of the two. Dual-element designs consist of a pleated-paper cartridge and a foam pre-cleaner. Some pre-cleaners are designed to be oiled. A mesh backing separates the oil on the pre-cleaner from the surface of the paper element. Others read "Do not oil." Identify the type of air cleaner on your engine before cleaning.

The Extended Life air filters offer four times the performance of standard filters used on ride-on mowers and garden tractors.

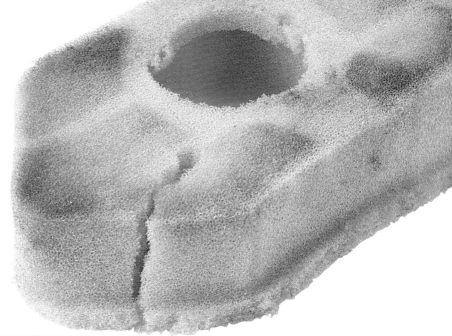

Don't wait until your air cleaner element looks like this to replace it. If your element has become permanently discolored or has begun to break down or tear, extend the life of your small engine by installing a new one.

A

Servicing a foam air cleaner

1. Loosen the screws or wing nuts that hold the air cleaner assembly in place (photo A). Disassemble.

2. Inspect the foam element. Replace it if it is torn or shows signs of considerable wear.

3. Saturate the new element with engine oil (photo B). Then, squeeze it to spread the oil throughout. Wrap foam in clean cloth and squeeze to remove excess oil.

4. Inspect the rubbery sealing gasket between the air cleaner and carburetor. Replace it if it is worn.

5. Reassemble and reinstall the air cleaner.

B

PAPER FILTERS AND TIPPING THE ENGINE

If your engine has a paper filter cartridge, remove it temporarily any time you are preparing to tip the engine on its side. You'll eliminate any chance that oil from the pre-cleaner will spill onto the paper and ruin it. To prevent debris from entering the carburetor, temporarily cover the carburetor opening with plastic.

Pleats in a paper element that are discolored, bent or water-damaged can no longer provide adequate air to the carburetor. Replace the element when it approaches this condition.

Servicing a pleated-paper or dual-element air cleaner

Dual-element air cleaners come in a variety of designs. Two of the most common are shown here.

1. With the cover removed, separate the pre-cleaner (if equipped) from the cartridge (photo C).

2. Tap the cartridge gently on a flat surface to remove any loose dirt. Inspect the element and replace it if it is heavily soiled, wet or crushed.

3. Inspect the pre-cleaner, if equipped. Note the mesh backing, designed to act as a barrier between the oily pre-cleaner and the pleated-paper element. Replace when soiled or worn or after 25 hours of use.

4. Look for oiling instructions on the pre-cleaner (photo D). *If directed,* lubricate the pre-cleaner with oil. NOTE: Not all foam pre-cleaners should be oiled.

5. Clean the cartridge housing with a dry cloth (photo E). Do not clean with solvents or compressed air.

6. Reassemble the air cleaner. If the pre-cleaner is the oiled type, take care to insert the mesh toward the paper element so that the paper is never exposed to the oil.

7. Reinstall, making sure that any tabs on the cartridge are in their slots on the engine housing. Gaps around the cartridge permit unfiltered air and damaging dirt particles to enter the engine.

ADDITIONAL MAINTENANCE

Tools & materials:
Socket wrench set, needlenose pliers, feeler gauge, spray solvent/lubricant.

Time required:
15-45 minutes.

Sometimes the standard box or socket wrench is not the ideal tool for the job. Some alternatives include: extension wrench head (A); six-sided box wrench (B); large offset box wrench (C); ratchet wrench (D); adjustable box wrench (E).

This section covers four additional tasks—testing engine compression, inspecting a crankcase breather, lubricating cables and linkages and tightening bolts—that will help you keep your engine in top condition. Take these steps when you're performing your seasonal maintenance, or any time your engine and equipment have been operating under a heavy load or dirty or dusty conditions.

Testing engine compression will tell you if you are getting the maximum power out of each piston stroke, without losing efficiency due to a leaky valve or other cylinder problems.

Inspecting a crankcase breather will ensure that crankcase gases are properly vented.

Lubricating cables and linkages should be done frequently during the season when your equipment sees its heaviest use. You'll avoid minor problems associated with binding controls or a sluggish governor.

Tightening bolts is necessary to ensure safe operation and to protect the engine block and equipment body.

Testing engine compression

When your engine has leaks around the valves or rings, compression of the air-fuel mixture suffers. When this happens, performance and efficiency can drop dramatically. A spin of the flywheel will tell you whether the compression in your engine is sufficient.

1. Disconnect the spark plug lead and secure it away from the spark plug. Remove the blower housing. Then, disconnect the brake pad or band, if equipped (see "Servicing the Brake," pages 122 to 127).

2. Spin the flywheel counter-clockwise by hand (photo A). If compression is adequate, the fly-wheel should rebound sharply. Weak or nonexistent rebound indicates poor compression (see "Trouble-shooting," pages 60 to 61, for a list of possible causes and remedies).

Inspecting a crankcase breather

Many engines contain a crankcase breather to vent gases that accumu-late in the crankcase. The breather (if equipped) is usually located over the valve chamber.

1. Remove the muffler or other parts to reach the breather. Then, loosen the breather retaining screws and remove the breather.

2. Make sure the tiny holes in the body are open. Use a feeler gauge to check the gap between

the fiber valve and the breather body (photo B). If a 0.045 in. feeler gauge can be inserted, replace the breather. Avoid using force or pressing on the fiber disc, and never disassemble the breather. If the breather is damaged, replace it. Replace the old gasket that fits between the breather and the engine body whenever you remove the breather.

Tightening bolts

Bolts on your engine must be tight at all times (photo D). If the bolts remain loose, parts can easily be damaged during engine operation.

Mounting bolts that attach the engine to the equipment can also loosen, leading to damage, such as a cracked engine block. Check these and all other accessible nuts and bolts during regular maintenance, and any time you sense excess vibration.

Lubricating cables and linkages

Control cables and linkages on the governor, flywheel brake and throttle can seize and may even throw off engine performance if they can't be moved freely. You can reduce bind-ing to a minimum and keep cables and linkages free of dirt and debris by spraying them occasionally with a solvent/lubricant (photo C).

Some mounting bolts must be grasped with a wrench from above and tightened with a second wrench from beneath the equipment. Others are self-tapping, and overtightening can damage the threads. Consult your authorized service dealer for the proper torque for each bolt on your engine, and use a torque wrench for final tightening.

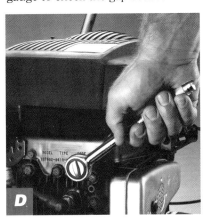

Basic Repair

Repair projects should always start with troubleshooting—the search for the source of a problem—starting with the most obvious or simple explanation and working toward the less obvious or more complex.

When you're troubleshooting a small engine problem, you need to rule out the various parts or systems as possible sources of the problem. It's important to work systematically to isolate the cause rather than skipping parts or systems that you believe are in good working order.

It's a lot like looking for a lost set of keys: often, they're in an "obvious" place that didn't seem worth checking. The solution is not to overlook things that seem obvious. They just might hold the keys.

For successful troubleshooting:

- Make sure you consider all symptoms carefully.

- Look for the cause, not just a cure for the symptoms.

- Gather as much information as possible. Knowing whether an engine was at top speed when it stopped running or whether it simply failed to start may make a difference when you're trying to identify the problem.

Remember that a simple solution is not always the correct one, or may be only a partial solution. Replacing a worn spark plug may get an engine running, but the real culprit may be a carburetor that is partially blocked. In this case, the problem will probably turn up again soon.

Common problems

Most four-stroke engine problems fall into one of these categories:

Engine won't start:

Fuel line problems

Carburetor problems

Ignition problems

Compression problems

Engine runs poorly:

Engine smokes

Engine overheats

Engine knocks

Engine misses under load

TROUBLESHOOTING

If this is the problem:	Ask this question:	If the answer is yes:

Engine won't start

(Fuel line)

Is the fuel tank empty? — Fill the fuel tank; if the engine is still hot, wait until it has cooled before filling the tank (see "Removing and Cleaning the Fuel Tank", page 71).

Is the shut-off valve closed? — Open the fuel shut-off valve (see "Removing and Cleaning the Fuel Tank," page 71).

Is the fuel diluted with water? — Empty the tank, replace the fuel and check for leaks in the fuel tank cap (see "Removing and Cleaning the Fuel Tank," page 71).

Is the fuel line or inlet screen blocked? — Disconnect the inlet screen from the engine and clean it, using compressed air. Do not use compressed air near the engine (see "Removing and Cleaning the Fuel Tank," page 71).

Is the fuel tank cap clogged or unvented? — Make sure the cap is vented and that air holes are not clogged (see "Removing and Cleaning the Fuel Tank," page 71).

(Carburetor)

Is the carburetor blocked? — Remove the spark plug lead and spark plug; pour a teaspoon of fuel directly into the cylinder; reinsert the spark plug and lead; start the engine; if it runs for a moment before quitting, overhaul the carburetor (see "Adjusting the Carburetor", pages 76 to 79).

Is the engine flooded? — Adjust the float in the fuel bowl, if adjustable; make sure the choke is not set too high (see "Adjusting the Carburetor", pages 76 to 79).

(Ignition)

Is the spark plug fouled? — Remove the spark plug; clean the contacts or replace the plug (see "Servicing Spark Plugs," pages 50 to 51).

Is the spark plug gap set incorrectly? — Remove the spark plug; reset the gap (see "Servicing Spark Plugs," pages 50 to 51).

Is the spark plug lead faulty? — Test the lead with a spark tester, then test the engine (see "Servicing Spark Plugs," pages 50 to 51).

Is the kill switch shorted? — Repair or replace the kill switch (see "Servicing the Brake," pages 122 to 127).

Is the flywheel key damaged? — Replace the flywheel key, re-torque the flywheel nut to proper specifications, then try to start the engine; if it still won't start, check the ignition armature, wire connections or, in some engines, the points (see "Replacing the Ignition," pages 100 to 103).

(Compression)

Are the valves, piston, cylinder or connecting rod damaged? — Perform a compression test (see "Additional Maintenance," pages 56 to 57); if the test indicates poor compression, inspect the valves, piston and cylinder for damage and repair them as needed (see "Removing Carbon Deposits," pages 108 to 111, and "Servicing the Valves," pages 112 to 121).

If this is the problem:	**Ask this question:**	**If the answer is yes:**

Engine runs poorly

Engine smokes

Is the fuel mixture too rich?   Adjust the carburetor (see "Adjusting the Carburetor," pages 76 to 79).

Is the air filter plugged?   Clean or replace the air cleaner (see "Servicing Air Cleaners," pages 52 to 55).

Engine overheats

Is the engine dirty?   Clean the engine (see "Removing Debris," pages 66 to 69).

Is the oil level low?   Add oil to the engine. NOTE: Never add oil to the gasoline for a four-stroke engine (see "Checking & Changing Oil," pages 46 to 49).

Are any shrouds or cooling fins missing or broken?   Install new parts as needed (see "Additional Tools, Parts & Supplies," pages 128 to 131).

Is the fuel mixture too lean?   Adjust the carburetor (see "Adjusting the Carburetor," pages 76 to 79).

Is there a leaky gasket?   Replace the gasket (see "Overhauling the Carburetor," pages 90 to 97).

Is the fuel tank vent or fuel tank screen plugged?   Clean the fuel tank vent and fuel tank screen (see "Removing and Servicing the Fuel Tank," pages 70 to 71).

Engine knocks

Does the combustion chamber contain excess carbon?   Clean carbon from the piston and head (see "Removing Carbon Deposits," pages 108 to 111).

Is the flywheel loose?   Inspect the flywheel and key; replace as needed (see "Inspecting the Flywheel & Key," pages 98 to 99).

Spark plug misses under load

Is the spark plug fouled?   Clean the spark plug (see "Cleaning and Inspecting a Spark Plug," page 51).

Is the spark plug faulty or gap incorrect?   Replace the spark plug or adjust the spark plug gap (see "Cleaning and Inspecting a Spark Plug," page 51).

Are the breaker points faulty?   Install a solid-state ignition (see "Replacing the Ignition," pages 100 to 103).

Is the carburetor set incorrectly?   Adjust the carburetor (see "Adjusting the Carburetor," pages 76 to 79).

Is the valve spring weak?   Replace the valve spring (see "Servicing the Valves," pages 112 to 121).

Is the valve clearance set incorrectly?   Adjust the valve clearance to recommended settings (see "Servicing the Valves," pages 112 to 121).

INSPECTING & CHANGING THE MUFFLER

Tools & materials:
Hammer, mallet, metal snips, pipe wrench, pin punch, slip-joint pliers, socket wrench.

Time required:
30 minutes.

One of the main sources of small engine noise is the hot gases that are forced out of the cylinder during each exhaust stroke. A muffler does a good job of reducing exhaust noise. But after a season or two, exhaust gases leave a layer of soot in the muffler that creates additional resistance to gases exiting the cylinder. When hard soot accumulates, when the exhaust emits excessive noise or when cracks or holes appear, don't try to repair the muffler. Once a muffler shows signs of deterioration, replace it. This section covers the procedures for removing, inspecting and replacing your muffler. It's an inexpensive and simple job if you take the proper precautions. Always wait for the engine to cool completely before handling the muffler. The muffler's surface can remain very hot and can easily cause a burn, even after the engine is stopped. A rusty muffler can cut you, especially if it crumbles during replacement. If any sharp edges are exposed, use slip-joint pliers to remove the muffler.

HOT! Keep your distance from the muffler and other engine parts until the engine has had plenty of time to cool.

How your muffler works

The force of exhaust gases as they rush through the small opening in the exhaust valve produces shock waves. It's the muffler's job to reduce noise by routing the exhaust through a series of perforated baffles and plates that break up the sound waves. The inside of the muffler also functions as a spark arrestor, preventing exhaust sparks from exiting and igniting dry grass, leaves or debris.

We quickly notice when a muffler is not doing its job. Even small cracks or holes in the muffler can result in a dramatic increase in engine noise.

When it's time to replace the muffler, use original manufacturer's equipment for safety and optimal engine performance.

Inspecting the muffler

1. Locate the muffler, which is usually near the cylinder head.

2. Check the outside of the muffler for signs of rust, dents, holes or cracks, any of which can restrict the exhaust and reduce the effectiveness of the muffler.

3. If there's soot near the exit hole, remove the muffler to check for soot inside.

Removing the muffler

The muffler body may be attached directly to the engine with mounting bolts or screwed into the engine body. On some mufflers, an extended pipe threads into the engine.

1. If the muffler is attached with mounting bolts and has locking tabs around the bolts, bend the tabs back far enough to fit a wrench over the bolt heads. Remove the bolts (photo A) and detach the muffler.

If the muffler screws directly into the engine, apply some penetrating oil to the threads (photo B) and let the oil work for several minutes. Tip the engine very slightly, if necessary, to allow the oil to reach the threads. NOTE: Don't tip the engine sharply. This can cause oil to drain into the carburetor and air cleaner.

Some mufflers are fastened with a threaded lock ring. Loosen it by tapping it counterclockwise with a hammer and pin punch. Then, grasp the muffler with slip-joint pliers and unscrew counterclockwise (photo C).

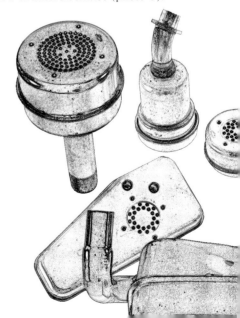

2. To check for soot, tap the muffler body with a mallet or on a hard surface (photo D). If the muffler is damaged or large quantities of soot cannot be dislodged, replace the muffler with original manufacturer's parts. If the muffler is in good condition, reattach it.

3. Don't overtighten the new muffler. If a lock ring is used, install it using a hammer and pin punch. NOTE: The smooth side of the lock ring must be against the cylinder in aluminum-block engines. The tooth side must be against the cylinder in cast-iron engines.

4. Brush the entire area to clear away dirt and debris. If left on the muffler, dried grass clippings and other debris can catch fire on the hot surface of the muffler.

Removing a rusty muffler

A very rusty muffler may collapse or crumble as you twist it with a wrench. There's no harm done as long as you take care not to damage muffler mounting threads in the engine block or other muffler fittings on the engine. If your muffler screws into the engine, cut the muffler body off with metal snips. Then, grasp the stem, using slip-joint pliers, and unscrew (photo E). If the muffler breaks off, leaving a connecting pipe attached to the engine, grasp the pipe with slip-joint pliers and unscrew (photo F).

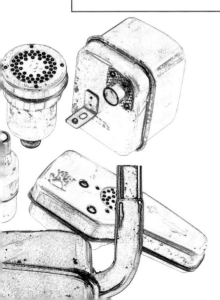

REMOVING *DEBRIS*

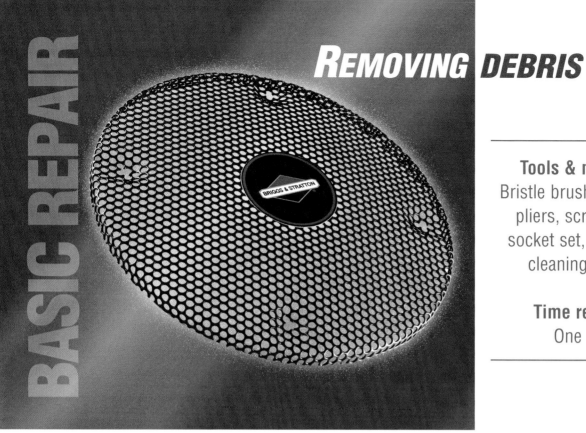

Tools & materials:
Bristle brush, needlenose pliers, screwdrivers, socket set, mild parts-cleaning solvent.

Time required:
One hour.

*G*rass and other debris may hardly seem like a critical repair issue for your small engine. But once it accumulates in between engine parts, it can cause a temporary loss of power or even permanent engine damage. Debris under the blower housing or in the cooling fins on the cylinder head can make an engine run too hot. Prolonged overheating may cause engine damage. Debris can also cause governor linkages to bind or prevent air from reaching the governor blade on a pneumatic governor, resulting in difficulty controlling engine speed. Inspect the blower housing and muffler area for debris each time you use your engine. If the screen over the blower housing is clogged, it's a good indication that debris has accumulated underneath as well. Remove the blower housing for a more thorough inspection and cleaning at the end of each season of use and more often if you operate your equipment in tall or wet grass.

Inspecting for debris

1. Start by disconnecting the spark plug lead and securing it away from the spark plug.

2. Snap off the plastic blower housing. If the housing is metal, you will need to remove a set of screws or bolts. On some models, removing the screws requires a star-shaped screwdriver or socket. A complete set of common sizes is available at hardware stores.

3. Clean the cooling fins, the inside of the blower housing and the flywheel fins, using a small bristle brush (photo A). Scrape dirt away gently, using a putty knife or bristle brush, taking care not to damage the housing or flywheel (photo B). To loosen stubborn grit, apply a light solvent, such as Briggs & Stratton All Purpose Cleaner, to the brush.

4. Dirt and debris on the fly-wheel cutting screen can lessen the engine's ability to cool itself. Clean the screen thoroughly with a brush (photo C).

A

B

C

5. Remove all debris by hand or with the knife and brush. Avoid using compressed air, which can force debris into less accessible engine parts.

6. Remove any debris from governor linkages, including the pneumatic governor vane, if so equipped (photo A). Then, make certain linkages are moving freely, using a light solvent to loosen remaining dirt and debris.

7. Check for debris around the brake assembly (photo B). Make sure the brake cable and linkage move freely.

8. Reattach the blower housing (photo C).

9. Reconnect spark plug.

Checking the stop switch

If your lawn mower stops unexpectedly while you're mowing around trees or bushes, you may have accidentally disconnected the stop switch wire, a short wire extending from the brake assembly to the ignition armature (photo D).

A disconnected stop switch wire may ground the ignition, preventing the spark plug from firing. Under ordinary conditions, the stop switch is designed to stop the engine any time you release the brake bail on the equipment handle.

You should be able to get the engine running again by pressing on the flexible metal tab on the stop switch and reattaching the wire. Take care not to break the wire as you twist it back into position.

D

Degreasing your engine

With your equipment in a well-ventilated area and the engine off, spray a degreasing agent, such as Briggs & Stratton Heavy-Duty Degreaser, liberally on greasy and dirt-encrusted surfaces (photo E). Wait 15 minutes to allow grease and dirt to break down. Wipe away the residue with a clean cloth (photo F). Hose the equipment surfaces (photo G), and allow them to dry completely before storing.

E

F

G

SERVICING THE FUEL TANK

Tools & materials:
Baster, flashlight,
fuel line clamp, screwdriver,
socket wrench.

Time required:
30 minutes.

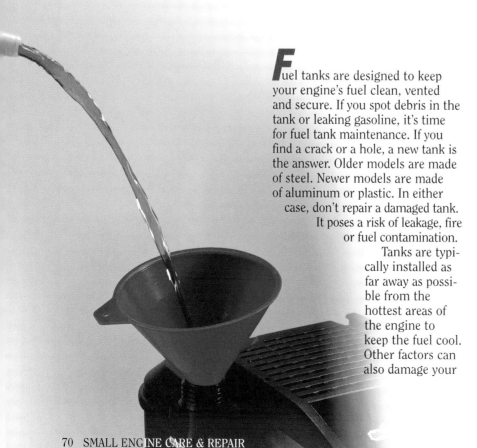

Fuel tanks are designed to keep your engine's fuel clean, vented and secure. If you spot debris in the tank or leaking gasoline, it's time for fuel tank maintenance. If you find a crack or a hole, a new tank is the answer. Older models are made of steel. Newer models are made of aluminum or plastic. In either case, don't repair a damaged tank. It poses a risk of leakage, fire or fuel contamination.

Tanks are typically installed as far away as possible from the hottest areas of the engine to keep the fuel cool. Other factors can also damage your tank. It can crack due to long-term exposure to hot sun and other elements, or if it is used to support weight from outside. Tanks often crack under such stress.

If you're replacing a fuel tank, use only parts recommended by the engine manufacturer. These parts will attach securely to your engine in the space provided.

Many fuel tanks are designed to use a vented fuel cap to prevent a vacuum from forming in the fuel line. If fuel is leaking from the cap, a properly fitted replacement cap can solve the problem. Refer to pages 12 and 13 for special safety instructions.

Your tank may also contain a fuel filter (see "Servicing the Fuel Filter," pages 72 to 73). Check it occasionally for debris.

Inside the fuel tank

Fuel tanks must be constructed of a noncorrosive material or coated with a corrosion-resistant layer to protect against the damaging effects of water, alcohol and salt. If the tank is designed to deliver fuel through a fuel line, a convex fuel filter may be located at the base of the tank, where fuel from the tank enters the fuel line. A filter can also be located outside the tank, midway along the fuel line.

If your tank must sustain excessive vibrations, you can install a labyrinth-equipped tank on some models. The labyrinth, available from your authorized service dealer, contains a set of baffles and/or a foam insert to reduce the sloshing and vaporization of fuel.

Fuel filter

Removing and cleaning the tank

1. Remove the spark plug lead and secure it away from the plug.

2. Use a fuel line clamp or other smooth-faced clamp to seal the fuel line where it attaches to the carburetor. Then, disconnect the line from the carburetor, hold the line over a bucket or fuel can

and release the clamp (photo A). Dispose of all fuel in a safe manner (see "Gasoline Use," page 73).

3. Check with a flashlight for debris and beads of light that indicate holes or cracks. Use a baster to remove loose debris (photo B). If you find damage, replace the tank with original manufacturer's equipment.

4. Inspect the fuel filter (see "Servicing the Fuel Filter," pages 72 to 73) for debris or deposits.

5. Reattach the fuel tank or install a new tank, fastening it firmly with the cap screws. This is a good opportunity to replace the fuel line and filter, using original manufacturer's equipment.

SERVICING THE FUEL FILTER

Tools & materials:
Flashlight, fuel line clamp, needlenose pliers.

Time required:
20 minutes.

A clean fuel filter strains the fuel before it reaches the carburetor and prevents foreign particles from clogging your engine. A dirty fuel filter can make the engine run too lean, with diminished performance and uneven operation. Other factors can cause these problems, but the fuel supply is one of the easiest to check.

Some filters are located inside the tank, others are fitted into the fuel line between the tank and the fuel pump. Most use either a mesh screen or pleated paper. The size of the holes in the filter will determine the largest particles that can get through the filter, and the number of holes will affect the amount of fuel that can flow through the filter.

Filters contain either a mesh screen or a pleated-paper element, and are rated by the size of the holes in the filtering material, expressed in microns (μ). Briggs & Stratton mesh screen filters are color-coded red for 150μ (microns), and white for 75μ. Pleated-paper filters, designed for use in the fuel tank, are typically contained in a clear plastic casing and rated 60μ. They consist of multiple folds that strain out particles suspended in the fuel.

The proper filter for your engine depends on the engine's design. Consult your authorized service dealer for the correct replacement filter.

Inspecting a fuel filter

Wear safety eyewear whenever removing or inspecting a filter to protect your eyes from liquid fuel or fuel vapors. Have a dry cloth handy to hold the filter and catch any dripping fuel.

If the filter is installed inside the tank, you will need to drain the tank before you can remove the filter for inspection or replacement.

1. Shut the fuel valve, if equipped. It's located at the base of the fuel tank, where the fuel line is attached. If your tank is not equipped with a fuel valve, clamp the fuel line, using a fuel line clamp.

2. If your filter is installed in the fuel line, remove the metal clips on each side of the filter, using needlenose pliers, and slide the filter out of the fuel line (photo A).

3. Shake the filter over a clean cloth to displace any remaining fuel, then use the cloth to wipe away any residue from the outside of the filter.

4. Keep the filter a safe distance from your face and look through one end (photo B). You should be able to see light shining through clearly from the other side. If debris is clogging the mesh screen or pleated paper or the inside of the casing, replace the filter.

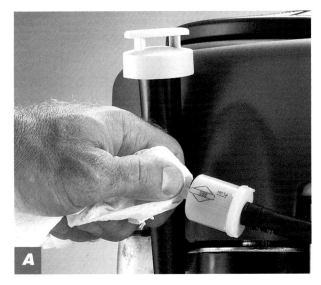

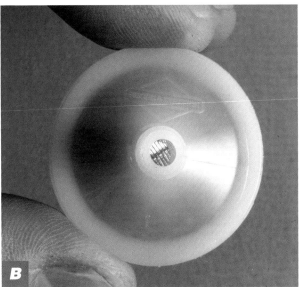

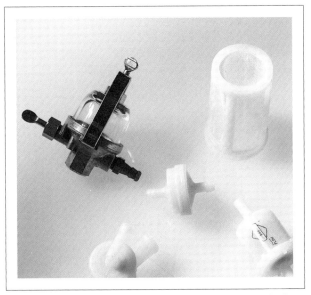

Heavier-duty small engines contain a fuel filter. If you don't find a filter mounted in your fuel line, look for one inside the fuel tank.

GASOLINE USE

Use only fresh unleaded gasoline in your small engine. Here are a few other tips for gasoline use in four-stroke small engines.

• Use gasoline with a 77 octane rating or higher for L-head engines and 85 or higher for overhead valve engines. Since small engines operate at relatively low compression ratios, knocking is seldom a problem, and using gasoline with a higher octane rating is unlikely to offer any benefit.

• Using gas that is over a month old and does not contain a gasoline stabilizer may result in hard starting and varnish formation. Drain the tank if fuel sits for more than a month. The Environmental Protection Agency recommends pouring old fuel into your car's gas tank. As long as the car's tank is at least half full, the old fuel will mix harmlessly with the new and will not affect your car engine.

• Four-stroke engines are used on most lawn mowers and large lawn equipment. NEVER use an oil-gasoline mixture in a four-stroke, since the engine has an independent oil supply. If you find an oil fill cap leading to the crankcase, you can be sure your engine is a four-stroke.

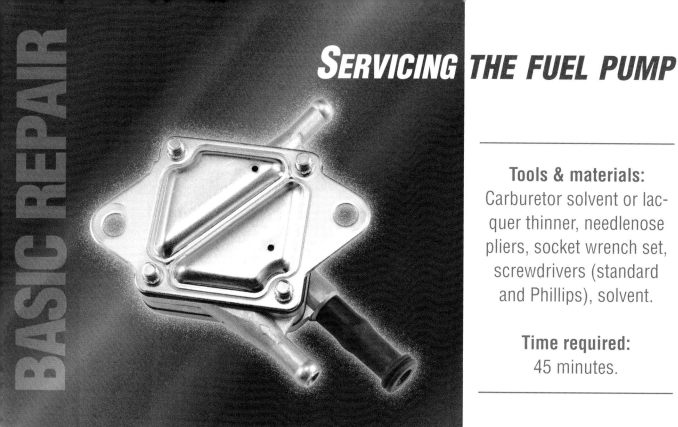

SERVICING THE FUEL PUMP

BASIC REPAIR

Tools & materials:
Carburetor solvent or lacquer thinner, needlenose pliers, socket wrench set, screwdrivers (standard and Phillips), solvent.

Time required:
45 minutes.

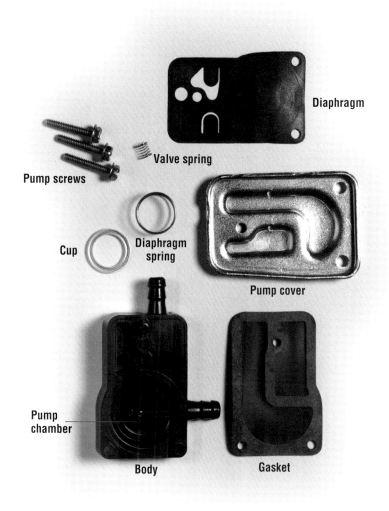

Diaphragm

Valve spring

Pump screws

Cup

Diaphragm spring

Pump cover

Pump chamber

Body

Gasket

A fuel pump is used when the fuel tank is mounted lower than the carburetor and cannot rely on gravity to carry fuel through the fuel line. Briggs & Stratton fuel pumps have either a plastic or a metal body and develop pressure using the vacuum in the crankcase, which is created by the motion of the piston. A fitting on the crankcase cover or the dipstick tube draws on the crankcase vacuum to create the pressure to pump fuel.

The fuel pump may be mounted on the carburetor, near the fuel tank or between the tank and carburetor.

Inspecting the pump

1. Turn off the fuel valve (if equipped) at the base of the fuel tank, where the fuel line is attached. If there is no fuel valve, stop the flow of fuel, using a fuel line clamp.

2. Loosen the mounting screws and remove the pump from the mounting bracket or carburetor (photo A).

3. Check for hairline cracks and other damage to the external surfaces of the pump. If the pump is damaged and has a metal body, discard the pump and install a replacement pump from the engine manufacturer (photo B).

Servicing the pump

You can service a plastic-body pump, using a manufacturer's repair kit to replace worn parts. A damaged metal-body pump must be replaced.

1. With the fuel valve closed or the line clamped, remove the mounting screws. Then, disconnect the fuel hoses, using needlenose pliers to loosen the clips. Remove the screws and disassemble the pump.

2. Inspect the body for cracks or other damage. Soak metal parts in all-purpose parts cleaner. The pump body may be soaked for up to 15 minutes (photo C).

3. Check the hoses for cracks, softening or hardening, and replace any faulty parts. Discard old gaskets, diaphragms and springs, and replace them with parts from an original manufacturer's repair kit.

Reinstalling the pump

1. Referring to the photo on page 74 (lower left), place the diaphragm spring and then the cup over the center of the pump chamber. Also insert a valve spring.

2. Install the diaphragm, gasket and cover and attach with pump screws. Tighten the screws to 10 to 15 in. lbs., using a torque wrench.

3. Attach the pump to the carburetor or mounting bracket, using the pump mounting screws

Metal-body pump

A

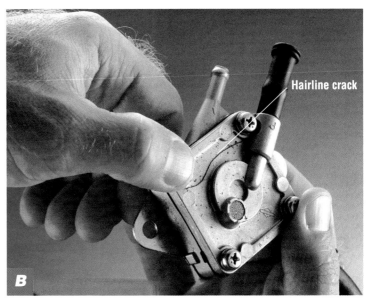

Hairline crack

B

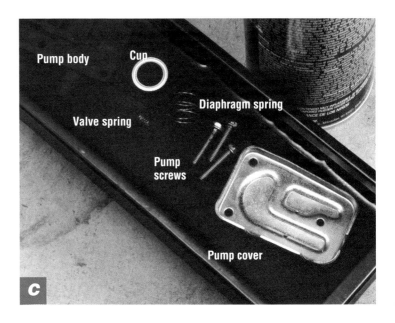

Pump body   Cup

Valve spring   Diaphragm spring

Pump screws

Pump cover

C

ADJUSTING THE CARBURETOR

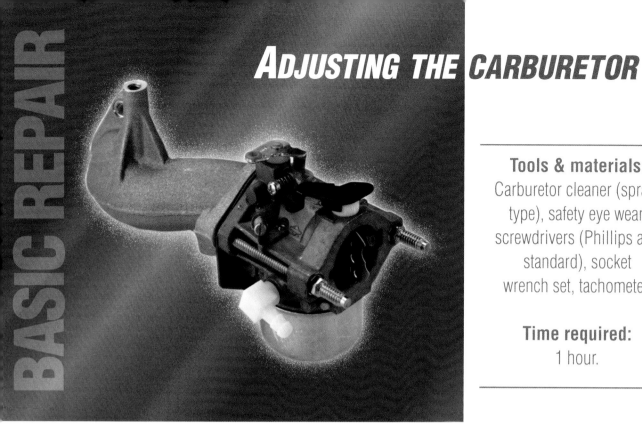

Tools & materials:
Carburetor cleaner (spray-type), safety eye wear, screwdrivers (Phillips and standard), socket wrench set, tachometer.

Time required:
1 hour.

*A*big part of ensuring a smooth-running engine is keeping your carburetor and linkages clean and well adjusted. The linkages attached to the carburetor's throttle and choke plates can bind or stick when dirty. Constant vibration and wear can affect the settings of the carburetor's mixture screws.

And with all of the grass, twigs and other debris that a small engine encounters, it's not surprising that even passages inside the carburetor eventually pay a price. Deposits inside the carburetor can clog fuel and air passages and reduce performance or stop the engine altogether.

Luckily, you can take care of many of these problems quickly and easily—often without even removing the carburetor from the engine. Commercially available carburetor cleaner comes in convenient spray cans for periodic cleaning both inside and outside the carburetor (photo A).

Troubleshooting a fuel supply problem

An engine that does not start or performs poorly may have a carburetor problem. The source of the problem may also be in the fuel valve, filter or pump. Start by checking these possible sources:

1. Remove the air cleaner and inspect the choke plate mounted on a shaft at the opening of the carburetor's throat (photo A). Check that the choke plate closes easily and completely. A choke that does not move freely or close properly can cause difficulties in starting.

2. Spray a small amount of carburetor cleaner on the shaft of a sluggish choke and into the venturi to loosen grit (photo A). Debris in the carburetor often causes performance problems.

3. Open the fuel valve (if equipped), located at the base of the fuel tank where the fuel line is attached. Remove the line and check for blockage (photo B). Fuel will not reach the carburetor if the fuel valve is closed.

4. If the engine is equipped with a fuel pump, make sure it operates properly (see "Servicing the Fuel Pump," pages 74 to 75).

5. Remove and inspect the spark plug. A wet plug may indicate over-choking, water in the fuel (see "Servicing the Fuel Tank," pages 70 to 71), or an excessively rich fuel mixture. A dry plug may indicate a plugged fuel filter (see "Servicing the Fuel Filter," pages 72 to 73), leaking mounting gaskets on either end of the carburetor, or a stuck or clogged carburetor inlet needle.

6. Pour a teaspoon of fuel into the spark plug hole (photo C). Screw the spark plug back in and start the engine. If it fires only a few times and then quits, assume a dry plug condition and consider the causes of a dry plug, listed in Step 5.

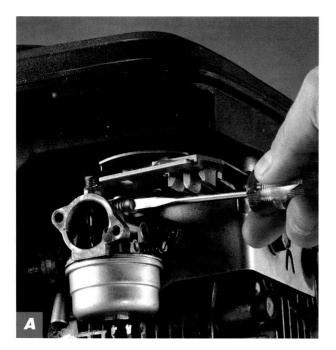

Adjusting the idle speed and mixture

On some float-type carburetors, you can adjust the air-fuel mixture and engine speed at idle. Check for an idle speed screw (see "Parts of the Carburetor," page 91), designed to keep the throttle plate from closing completely, and an idle mixture screw that limits the flow of fuel at idle. If your carburetor contains these screws, proceed below.

1. With the engine off, remove the air filter and air cartridge.

2. Locate the idle mixture screw and turn it clockwise until the needle lightly touches the seat. Then, turn the screw counterclockwise 1½ turns.

3. If your carburetor has a main jet adjustment screw at the base of the float bowl, turn the screw clockwise until you feel it just touch the seat inside the emulsion tube. Then, turn the screw counterclockwise 1 to 1½ turns. Replace the air cleaner assembly and start the engine for final carburetor adjustments.

4. Run the engine for five minutes at half throttle to bring it to its operating temperature. Then, turn the idle mixture screw slowly clockwise until the engine begins to slow

(photo A). Turn the screw in the opposite direction until the engine again begins to slow. Finally, turn the screw back to the midpoint.

5. Using a tachometer to gauge engine speed (photo B), set the idle speed screw to bring the engine to 1750 RPM for aluminum-cylinder engines or 1200 RPM for engines with a cast-iron cylinder sleeve.

6. With the engine running at idle (photo D), hold the throttle lever against the idle speed screw to bring the engine speed to "true idle." Then, repeat the idle mixture screw adjustments from Step 4 to fine-tune the mixture (photo C).

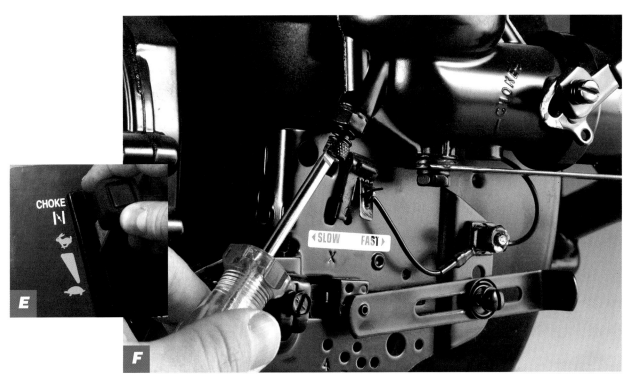

Adjusting the high speed mixture

Some older carburetors contain a high speed mixture screw, near the throttle plate and opposite the idle speed screw. Under load, the high speed circuit increases air flow through the throat. Setting the high speed mixture involves running the engine until it is warm, stopping it to adjust the high speed mixture and then restarting for final adjustments.

1. Run the engine for five minutes at half throttle to bring it to its operating temperature. Then, stop the engine.

2. Locate the high speed mixture screw and turn it clockwise until the needle just touches the seat. Then, turn the screw counterclockwise 1¼ to 1½ turns.

3. Restart the engine and set the throttle position to HIGH or FAST (photo E). Turn the high speed or main jet screw clockwise until the engine begins to slow. Then, turn the screw the other way until the engine begins to slow. Turn the screw back to the midpoint (photo F).

4. Once adjusted, check engine acceleration by moving the throttle from idle to fast. The engine should accelerate smoothly. If necessary, readjust mixture screws.

Adjusting the choke linkage

1. Remove the air cleaner and locate the choke lever on the engine or on the remote engine speed controls.

2. Move the equipment controls to FAST or HIGH (photo G). Loosen the cable mounting bracket to allow movement of the cable casing.

3. Move the cable casing so the choke is closed. Tighten the cable mounting screw (photo H) and check the motion of the control lever. Repeat the steps, as necessary, until the cable moves freely.

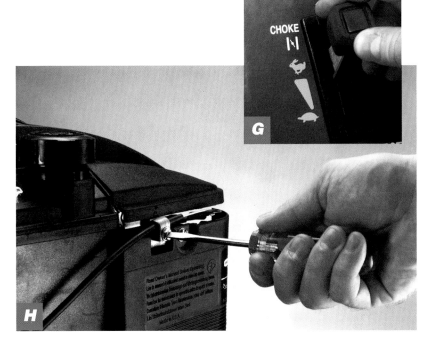

ADJUSTING THE GOVERNOR

Tools & materials:
Standard screwdriver,
combination wrench set,
socket wrench set,
tang bending tool.

Time required:
45 minutes.

The tang bending tool is the most common tool for setting governor spring tension. It's a simple metal lever with forked ends for bending the tabs, or tangs, on the governor and other engine parts.

A properly adjusted governor can maintain a steady engine speed regardless of changes in the terrain and other conditions that increase the work of the engine. These conditions are known as the "load." When engine speed starts to rise or fall in response to a change in the load, the governor responds, opening or closing the throttle. If you adjust engine speed manually, using the equipment controls, the governor's job is to maintain the new setting.

Your engine contains either a pneumatic governor or a mechanical governor (see "Governor System,"

pages 30 to 31). Remove the blower housing to determine which one your engine uses. Pneumatic governor linkages connect to a pivoting air vane next to the flywheel. On a mechanical governor, the linkages connect to a governor shaft (see photo, right).

For either type, follow the steps in these pages to adjust your governor for best performance. NOTE: Governor adjustment procedures vary widely depending on the make and model of the engine. Check with your authorized service dealer for the speed settings for your equipment.

Parts of the mechanical governor

1. Engine speed control. Moving this lever to a higher speed setting opens the throttle indirectly by pulling on the governor gear bracket.

2. Governor gear bracket. The bracket pivots, increasing tension on the governor spring.

3. Governor spring. Tension on the spring pulls on the governor lever in an effort to open the throttle plate.

4. Governor lever. The lever pivots, pulling on the throttle linkage and applying pressure to the governor shaft.

5. Governor shaft. The shaft links the governor linkages and levers to the governor cup and other parts inside the crankcase.

Crankshaft

6. Throttle linkage. The linkage tugs on the throttle lever.

7. Throttle lever. The lever opens the throttle plate, allowing more air-fuel mixture into the combustion chamber, causing engine speed to increase.

8. Governor gear. Increased engine speed causes governor gear to spin faster and flyweights to fly outward.

9. Flyweights. Movement of the flyweights applies pressure to the governor cup.

10. Governor cup. Governor cup causes the governor lever to pivot.

Spark plug lead

Choke control

Inspecting the governor

1. With the spark plug lead disconnected and secured away from the spark plug, check that the governor linkages are attached and move freely by pulling gently on the throttle lever. This should stretch the governor spring while pressing on the governor lever (photo A). If not, check that the governor spring and the link to the governor lever are properly attached to the throttle lever.

2. Springs and linkages that are not attached may be reconnected if they are in good condition. Twist them carefully into place to ensure that the delicate springs and linkages aren't permanently bent or stretched. Do not use pliers or other tools to bend or distort links or springs. Replace the governor spring if it is overstretched (photo B) and replace the linkages if they appear worn.

Governor lever arm

Hunting and surging

Your engine may race or slow intermittently even when the load and the speed control settings are unchanged. Follow the steps below to determine whether the source of this erratic engine behavior—known as "hunting and surging" is the carburetor or the governor.

1. Check that springs and linkages move freely and that the governor spring is inserted properly on the governor lever arm (photo A). On a mechanical governor, perform a static governor adjustment (opposite).

2. Run your engine at each of its speed settings to determine when hunting and surging occur. If the problem crops up at "true idle" (when the throttle lever is against the idle speed screw or stop), the air-fuel mixture is the likely cause. An air leak or debris in the carburetor is probably causing the air-fuel mixture to fluctuate. Remove and clean your carburetor (see "Overhauling the Carburetor," pages 90 to 97).

3. If hunting and surging occur at top no-load speed, run the following test. Move the throttle lever so the throttle plate is in the open position. If hunting and surging continue, the problem is probably in the carburetor. Clean and adjust the carburetor (see "Overhauling the Carburetor," pages 90 to 97). If hunting and surging is eliminated by opening the throttle, lubricate the governor linkage to eliminate any resistance and binding. If hunting

and surging persist, replace the governor spring(s) and retest.

4. Some engines have a separate "governed idle" spring and governed idle adjusting screw to prevent stalls under light loads. If hunting and surging occurs under light load, run the following test. Look for an idle speed screw, a stop screw on top of the carburetor, designed to prevent the throttle from closing completely. Hold the throttle lever against the idle speed screw and increase the governed idle speed by turning the screw slowly clockwise. If hunting and surging stop, replace the idle spring and linkage and reset the governed idle speed. If hunting and surging continue, clean and adjust the carburetor (see "Overhauling the Carburetor," pages 90 to 97).

Adjusting the "static" setting on a mechanical governor

The following procedure eliminates play in a mechanical governor between the governor crank—the arm that protrudes from the crankcase—and governor system components inside the crankcase. This procedure does not apply if your engine has a pneumatic governor.

1. Loosen the clamp bolt on the governor crank until the governor lever moves freely (photo C).

2. Move the throttle plate linkage until the throttle plate is wide open (photo D). (To find the wide-open position, first position the throttle lever against the idle speed screw or a fixed stop plate. The throttle is wide open when it is all the way in the opposite direction.) Note the governor arm's direction of rotation as you move the throttle plate to the wide-open position. This is important for the next step.

3. With the throttle plate wide open, use a nut driver or wrench to turn the governor shaft in the same direction that the governor arm traveled (photo E).

4. Hold the linkage and governor crank and tighten the governor arm clamp bolt (photo F). Move the linkage manually to make sure there is no binding.

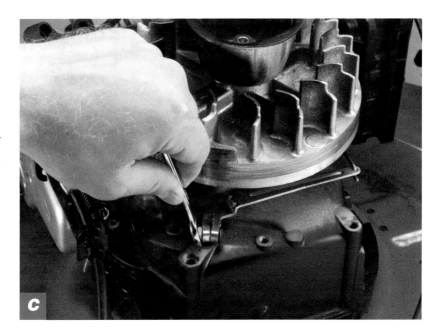

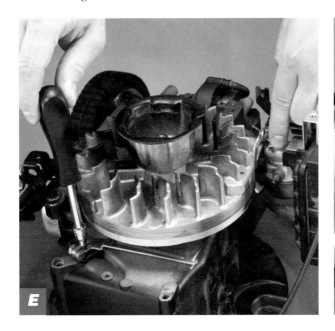

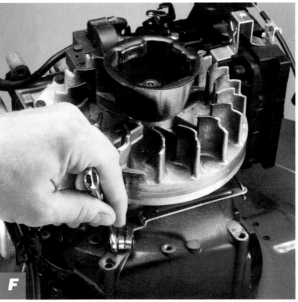

ADJUSTING GOVERNED IDLE

Some engines contain a shorter, smaller, "secondary" governor spring to discourage stalls when the engine is operating at idle under a light load. Under these conditions, the secondary spring keeps the engine at a "governed idle" speed slightly above its true idle speed. The idle speed screw is always set at less than the engine's governed idle speed. The procedure for adjusting governed idle varies depending on the engine model. Consult your owner's manual for the procedure for your model.

Keep in mind that the secondary spring affects all governor settings. If the governor on your engine has a secondary spring, you need to adjust the governed idle before setting the engine's top no-load speed.

Multiple governor spring holes

A

Governor adjustment screw

B

Tang bending and other adjustment methods

The tang bending tool pictured on page 80 (bottom) is the most common tool for governor spring adjustment. It's a simple metal lever with forked ends used for grasping and bending the tabs, or tangs, on the governor lever, spring anchor and other engine parts (see photo, page 81). Bending a tang increases or decreases the extension of the governor springs.

If the governor lever has multiple spring holes (photo A), you can increase top no-load speed by selecting a hole that is farther from the pivot point on the governor lever. On some engines, an adjustment screw alters governor spring tension, increasing or decreasing top no-load speed (photo B). Fine adjustments may still require the use of a tang bending tool (photos D, E and F).

Setting top no-load speed

If your engine races when you set your controls to HIGH, you need to reduce the engine's top speed under no-load conditions. Ask your authorized service dealer for the proper top no-load speed setting for your model. (If your governor contains two springs, skip to "Setting Dual-Spring Top No-Load Speed," below). The most common method for adjusting top no-load speed is to use a tang bending tool (see "Tang Bending and Other Adjustment Methods," left) to bend the spring anchor tang to stretch or relax the spring.

1. Attach the Tiny Tach to the engine's white ground wire with the alligator clip. The red wire should be wrapped around the spark plug lead (photo C). Run the engine for five minutes so it reaches its operating temperature.

2. Place the equipment on a hard, smooth surface with the engine running and the controls set to HIGH. Decrease top no-load speed by bending the tang toward the governor spring, until the manufacturer's specified speed setting is attained (photo D). Increase top no-load speed by lengthening the spring.

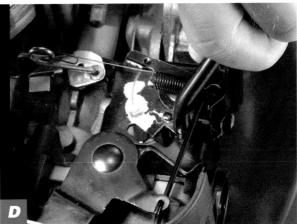

3. If your engine has a mechanical governor, proceed with the static governor adjustment (see "Adjusting the 'Static' Setting on a Mechanical Governor," page 83).

Setting dual-spring top no-load speed

If your governor contains two springs, the smaller, shorter spring is the secondary spring and must be adjusted to prevent stalls.

1. Attach a tachometer to the engine. With the engine running, bend the secondary spring tang (see "Tang Bending and Other Adjustment Methods," left) so there is no tension on the secondary spring (photo E).

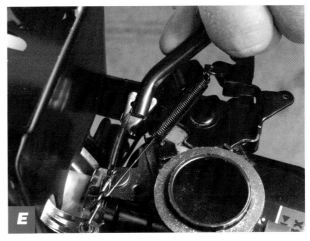

2. Bend the primary governor spring tang until the engine speed is 200 rpm below the manufacturer's specified top no-load speed (photo F).

3. Bend the secondary governor spring tang until the engine reaches its top no-load speed. Ask your authorized service dealer for the top no-load speed setting for your engine.

4. If your engine has a mechanical governor, proceed with the static governor adjustment (see "Adjusting the 'Static' Setting on a Mechanical Governor," page 83).

REPLACING THE REWIND

Tools & materials:
needlenose pliers,
power drill,
socket wrench set.

Time required:
45 minutes.

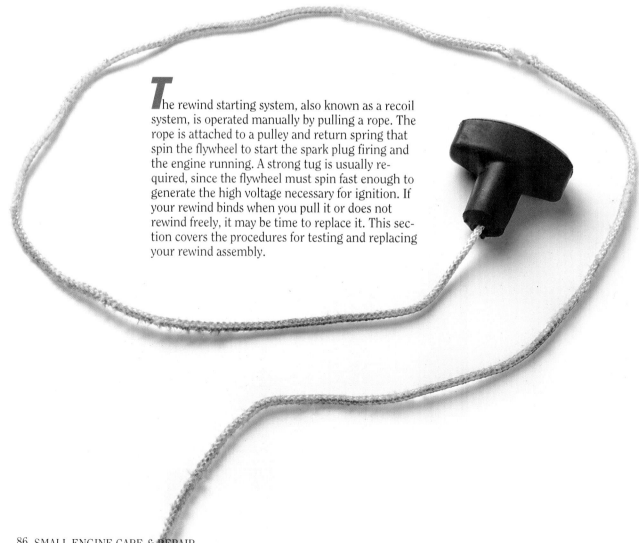

The rewind starting system, also known as a recoil system, is operated manually by pulling a rope. The rope is attached to a pulley and return spring that spin the flywheel to start the spark plug firing and the engine running. A strong tug is usually required, since the flywheel must spin fast enough to generate the high voltage necessary for ignition. If your rewind binds when you pull it or does not rewind freely, it may be time to replace it. This section covers the procedures for testing and replacing your rewind assembly.

Testing the rewind

If you discover any of the following conditions, replace the entire rewind assembly.

1. Pull the rope slowly (photo A). If the system is noisy, binds or feels rough, the return spring, pulley or rope may be jammed. If the crankshaft doesn't turn, the ratcheting mechanism isn't engaging.

2. Once the rope is all the way out, check for fraying and wear along its entire length.

3. Let the rope rewind slowly. If it fails to rewind, the pulley may be binding or the return spring may be broken, disengaged or worn.

Replacing the rewind

On some engines, the rewind is spot-welded or riveted to the top of the engine shroud. On others, it is attached with nuts or bolts.

1. Loosen the appropriate bolts and remove the blower housing (see "Removing Debris," pages 66 to 67).

2. Remove the nuts or bolts on the rewind (if equipped) or drill out the rivets or spot welds with a 3/16" bit, drilling only far enough to loosen them (photo B).

3. Install a replacement rewind from the original engine manufacturer. Insert the mounting bolts from inside the blower housing so that the bottoms come through the top of the shroud. Place the replacement rewind over the bolts and fasten a washer and nut securely on each bolt (photo C).

> ### REWIND SAFETY
>
> A rewind assembly contains a pulley and spring that retract the rope after each pull. Disassembling a rewind is best left to a small engine technician. The project requires special care and safety precautions because of the risk of serious injury from a spring or other flying parts.

ADVANCED REPAIR

The systems and techniques in this section are more complex than those described in the Basic Repair section. But they're well within your reach now that you have some basic repair projects under your belt. The same basic principles apply.

If an advanced repair task is new to you, start by reviewing "Troubleshooting" (pages 60 to 61) and "Safety" (pages 12 to 13).

Here are a few of the subjects you should review to prepare for the projects in this section:

- Before you clean your carburetor, review the basics of carburetor operation (see "Fuel System," pages 24 to 25).

- Before you replace the ignition, you should have some knowledge of how electricity is generated (see "Ignition System," pages 26 to 27).

- Before removing carbon deposits, it's helpful to understand the source of carbon deposits in the engine (see "Compression System" and "Fuel System," pages 20 to 25, and "Lubrication & Cooling System," pages 28 to 29).

- Before servicing the valves, review the mechanics of compression (see "Compression System," pages 20 to 23).

- Before servicing a brake or stop switches, review the principles of the flywheel brake (see "Braking System," pages 32 to 33).

The background provided in these system sections will help you get through the advanced repairs projects with no trouble. If you're concerned about special issues that pertain to your engine, contact an authorized service dealer. The technicians there can offer you helpful advice specific to your engine make and model.

If you have experience in basic repair and confidence in your ability, you can take on these tasks by yourself:

Inspecting the Flywheel & Key, pp. 98-99

Overhauling the Carburetor, pp. 90-97

Testing the Electrical System, pp. 104-107

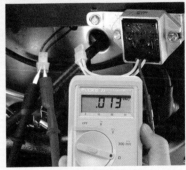

Replacing the Ignition, pp. 100-103

Servicing the Valves, pp. 112-121

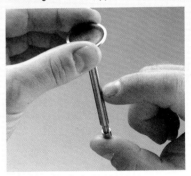

Removing Carbon Deposits, pp. 108- 111

Servicing the Brake, pp. 122-127

OVERHAULING THE CARBURETOR

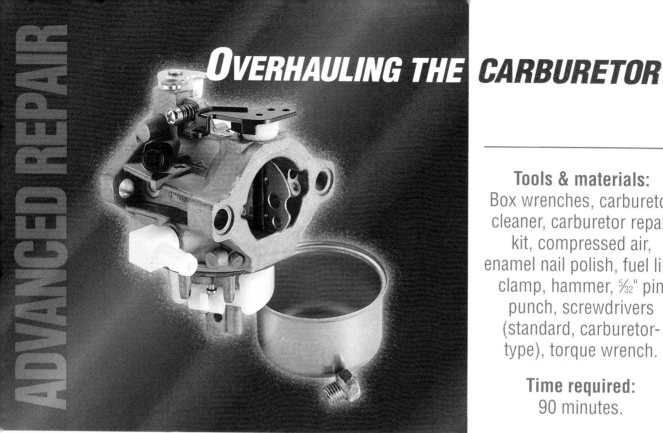

Tools & materials:
Box wrenches, carburetor cleaner, carburetor repair kit, compressed air, enamel nail polish, fuel line clamp, hammer, 5/32" pin punch, screwdrivers (standard, carburetor-type), torque wrench.

Time required:
90 minutes.

Carburetor rebuild kit

Most carburetor problems are caused by dirt particles, varnish and other deposits that block the narrow fuel and air passages inside. Gaskets and O-rings are also common sources of problems. They eventually shrink, causing fuel and air leaks that lead to poor engine performance.

If you're doing a rebuild, you'll need to purchase the repair kit for your carburetor, which includes replacement gaskets and other necessary parts. While you're

at it, check the price of a complete replacement carburetor for your engine. In some cases, it may be more cost-effective to install a new one.

If you decide to rebuild, you will also need carburetor cleaner, a clean work surface and, ideally, a source of compressed air for blowing out loosened debris and solvent.

The design of your carburetor depends on the size of the engine and the application. Engines designed for lawn tractors require a precisely tuned carburetor with a choke and idle mixture system. Walk-behind mower engines operate well without these design enhancements. This section offers directions for cleaning and adjusting a range of carburetor types. Yours may look different and may require fewer steps.

Parts of the carburetor

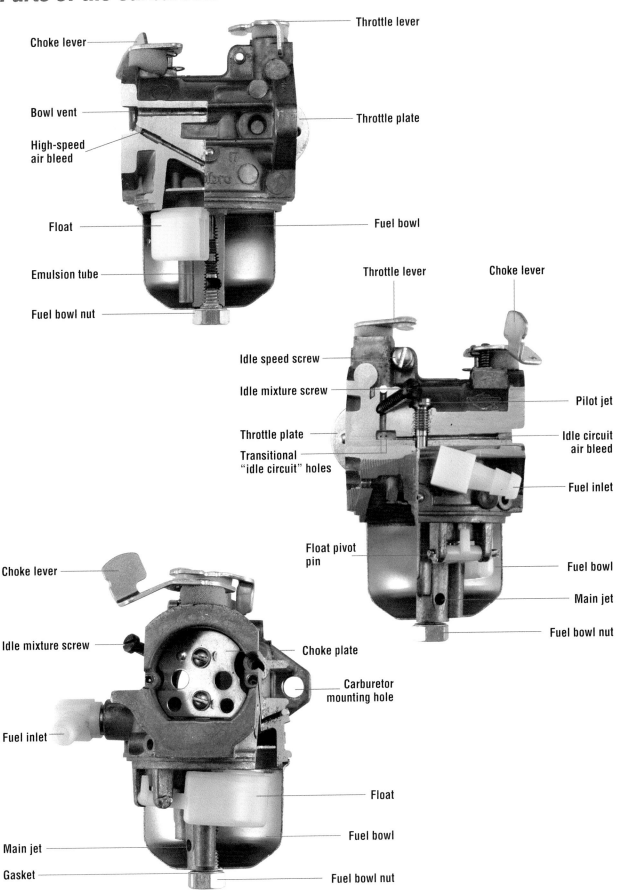

Choke lever

Throttle lever

Bowl vent

Throttle plate

High-speed air bleed

Float

Fuel bowl

Emulsion tube

Fuel bowl nut

Throttle lever

Choke lever

Idle speed screw

Idle mixture screw

Pilot jet

Throttle plate

Idle circuit air bleed

Transitional "idle circuit" holes

Fuel inlet

Float pivot pin

Fuel bowl

Main jet

Fuel bowl nut

Choke lever

Idle mixture screw

Choke plate

Carburetor mounting hole

Fuel inlet

Float

Fuel bowl

Main jet

Gasket

Fuel bowl nut

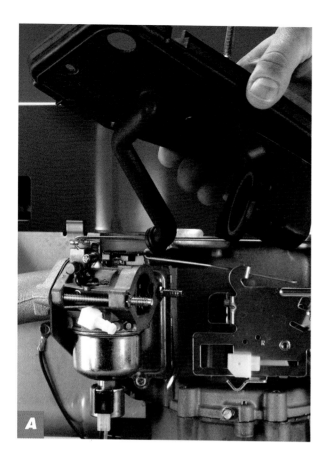

A

WORKING WITH SOLVENT

Carburetor cleaner is a powerful solvent that can harm carburetor parts—especially plastic parts—if they are soaked for too long. A carburetor should be soaked for no more than 15 minutes. Rubber parts, such as seals, O-rings and pump diaphragms, should never be exposed to carburetor cleaner and should always be removed before soaking.

Use only compressed air and carburetor cleaner to clear clogged passages or tiny meter holes in the carburetor. It may be tempting to ream or drill these holes and passages. Never do so. They are precisely sized and may be permanently damaged if any solid material, such as a wire or drill bit, is inserted.

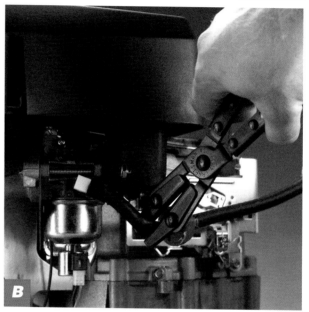

B

Removing the carburetor

1. Disconnect the spark plug lead and secure it away from the spark plug. Then, remove the air cleaner assembly (photo A).

2. Turn off the fuel valve at the base of the fuel tank. If your engine does not contain a fuel valve, use a fuel line clamp to prevent fuel from draining out of the tank while the carburetor is disconnected from the engine (photo B).

3. Some carburetors contain an electrical device at the base of the fuel bowl to control afterfire (photo C). Disconnect the device, known as an anti-afterfire solenoid, by removing the wire connector from the solenoid's receptacle.

4. With the carburetor still connected to the governor, unfasten the carburetor mounting bolts. If a connecting pipe joins the carburetor to the engine block (photo C), first remove the pipe mounting bolts. Then, disconnect the carburetor from the pipe by removing the nuts and sliding the carburetor off the studs.

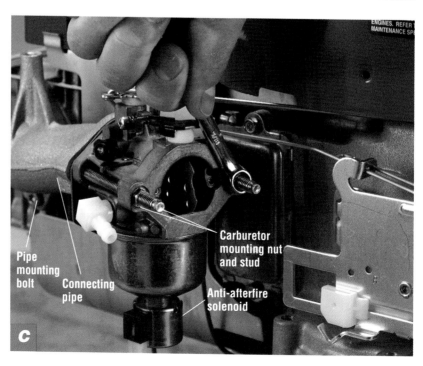

Pipe mounting bolt

Connecting pipe

Carburetor mounting nut and stud

Anti-afterfire solenoid

C

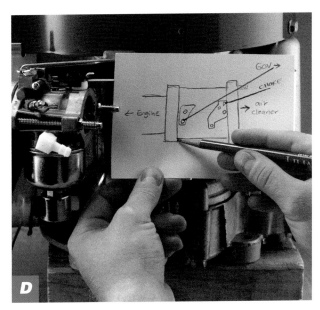

5. Sketch the governor spring positions before disconnecting them (photo D) to simplify reattachment. Then, disconnect the governor springs and remove the carburetor, taking special care not to bend or stretch links, springs or control levers.

Disassembling a float-type carburetor

Your carburetor contains a small amount of fuel. Prepare a clean bowl to catch dripping fuel and store small parts. During disassembly, inspect the bowl for dirt and debris to determine the condition of your carburetor.

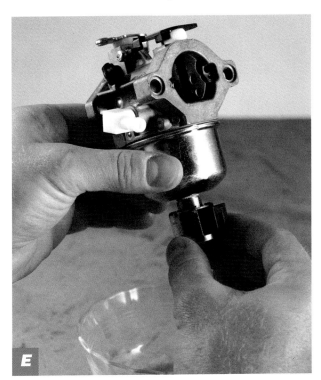

1. Remove the fuel bowl from the carburetor body (photo E). The fuel bowl may be attached with either a bolt or the high-speed mixture screw.

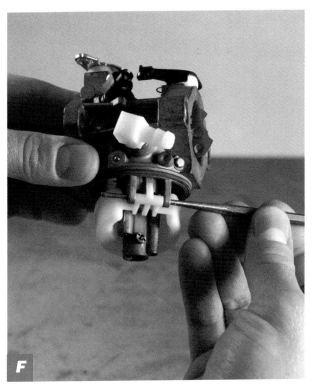

2. Push the hinge pin out of the carburetor body (photo F) with a small pin or pin punch. Take care to tap only the pin to avoid damaging the carburetor body.

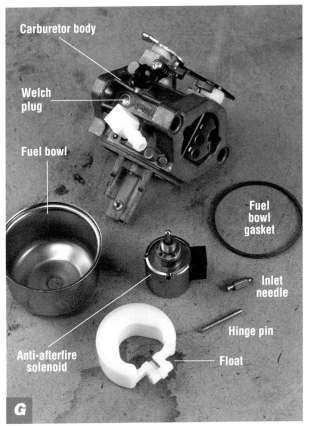

Carburetor body

Welch plug

Fuel bowl

Fuel bowl gasket

Inlet needle

Hinge pin

Anti-afterfire solenoid

Float

3. Remove the float assembly, inlet needle valve and fuel bowl gasket (photo G).

(continued on next page)

4. If your carburetor contains an idle mixture screw, remove it along with the spring (photo A).

5. Rotate the throttle plate to the closed position, remove the throttle plate screws and the throttle plate (photo B).

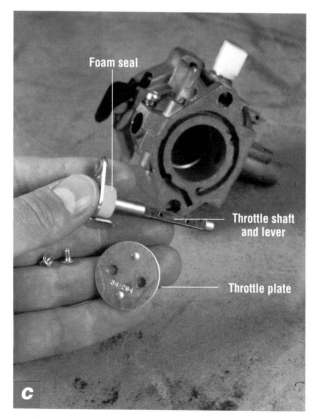

Foam seal

Throttle shaft and lever

Throttle plate

Welch plug

6. Remove the throttle plate shaft and foam seal (photo C). Then, remove the choke plate and choke shaft and felt or foam washer in the same manner.

7. Use your carburetor repair kit to identify replaceable welch plugs (photo D). These seals cover openings in the carburetor left over from machining. Insert a sharpened ⁵⁄₃₂" pin punch at the edge of each plug to be removed and tap cleanly to free the plug.

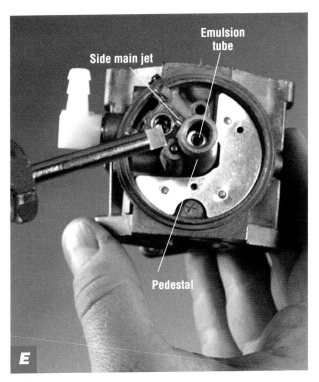

Side main jet

Emulsion tube

Pedestal

E

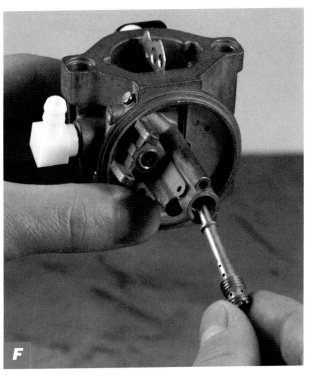

F

8. Unscrew the main jet from the side of the carbure-tor pedestal (if equipped). Then, unscrew the emulsion tube; it may be screwed in tight. A carburetor screwdriver is the best tool for the job. It's designed to fit the slot in the head of the emulsion tube (photo E) so that you won't damage the threads inside the pedestal or the tube itself as you loosen it.

9. Remove the emulsion tube (photo F).

Inspect the carburetor

1. Soak metal and plastic carbu-retor parts in all-purpose parts cleaner for no more than 15 minutes to remove grit (photo G). Or, wear-ing safety glasses, spray the parts with carburetor cleaner. Then, wipe away solvent and other residue thoroughly, using a clean cloth. Never use wire or tools. They can damage or further obstruct plugged openings.

2. Inspect all components and use additional carburetor cleaner to loosen stubborn grit and to clear obstructions.

3. Replace any parts that are damaged or permanently clogged.

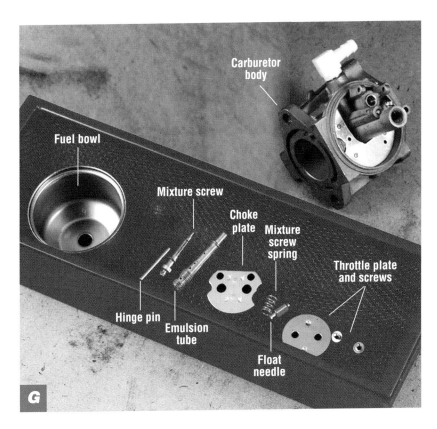

Carburetor body

Fuel bowl

Mixture screw

Choke plate

Mixture screw spring

Throttle plate and screws

Hinge pin

Emulsion tube

Float needle

G

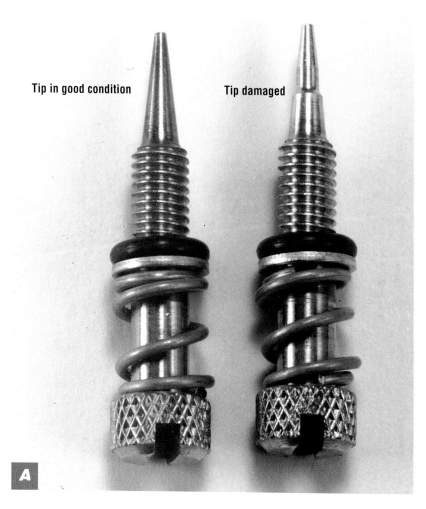

Tip in good condition   **Tip damaged**

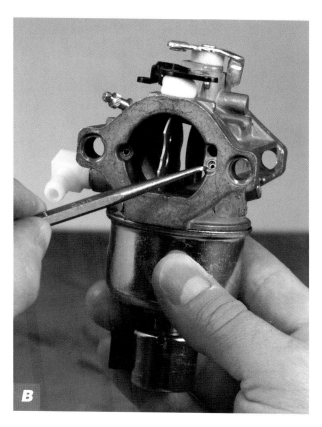

A

Inspecting mixture screws

Brass mixture screws control the air-fuel mixture at high speed and at idle. Overtightening can damage the tip of the screw so that proper adjustment is no longer possible (photo A). Remove any nonmetal parts and soak mixture screws in carburetor cleaner for 15 minutes. Then, inspect them carefully for wear. Replace a mixture screw if the tip is bent or contains a ridge.

Compensating for high altitude

Small engines are set at the factory to operate at average atmospheric pressure. If you live at a high altitude, you may need to modify the carburetor to ensure adequate air or fuel intake. Depending on your model, you will need to remove the small metal fitting near the choke plate, known as the main jet air bleed (photo B) or replace the fixed main jet (photo C) with one designed for high elevations. Ask your authorized service dealer for additional details on the necessary adjustments for your area.

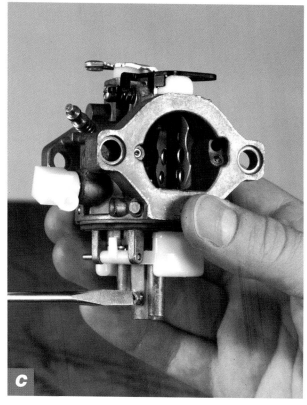

B

C

Reassembling the carburetor

1. Install new welch plugs from your repair kit, using a pin punch slightly smaller than the outside diameter of the plug (photo D). Tap on the punch with a hammer until the plug is flat (strong blows with the hammer will cause the plug to cave in). Then, seal the outside edge of the plug with enamel nail polish.

2. Assemble the choke by inserting the return spring inside the foam seal and sliding the spring and seal assembly onto the choke shaft. Plastic choke plates have a stop catch at one end of the spring; metal plates have a notch to hold the hook at one end of the spring.

3. Insert the choke shaft into the carburetor body and engage the return spring. If the choke lever uses a detent spring to control the choke plate position, guide the spring into the notched slot on the choke lever. Place the choke plate on the shaft with the single notch on the edge toward the fuel inlet. Lift the choke shaft and lever up slightly and turn counterclockwise until the stop on the lever clears the spring anchor. Push the shaft down.

4. Insert the choke plate into the choke shaft or attach it with screws so that the dimples face the fuel inlet side of the carburetor. The dimples help hold and align the choke shaft and plate.

5. Install the throttle shaft seal with the sealing lip down in the carburetor body until the top of the seal is flush with the top of the carburetor. Turn the shaft until the flat side is facing out. Attach the throttle plate to the shaft with the screws so that the numbers on the throttle plate face the idle mixture screw and the dimples face in.

D

6. Install the inlet needle seat with the groove down, using a bushing driver. Then, install the inlet needle on the float and install the assembly in the carburetor body.

7. Insert the hinge pin and center pin. Then, install the rubber gasket on the carburetor and attach the fuel bowl, fiber washer and bowl nut.

Attaching the carburetor and air cleaner assembly

1. Position the carburetor so the beveled edge fits into the fuel intake pipe and attach the carburetor with nuts or bolts, as required (photo E), leaving these fasteners loose for final tightening with a torque wrench. Consult your authorized service dealer for the proper tightening torque.

2. Install the air cleaner assembly, making certain that the tabs on the bottom of the air cleaner are engaged.

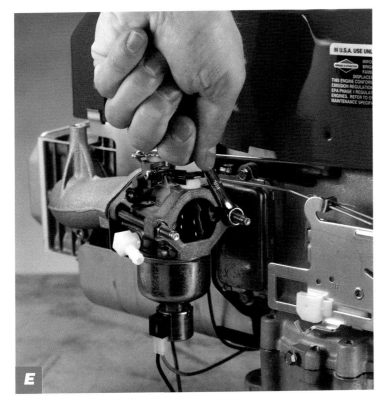

E

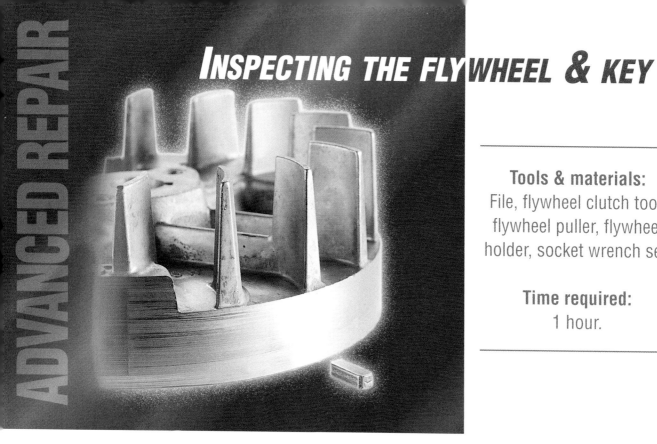

INSPECTING THE FLYWHEEL & KEY

Tools & materials:
File, flywheel clutch tool, flywheel puller, flywheel holder, socket wrench set.

Time required:
1 hour.

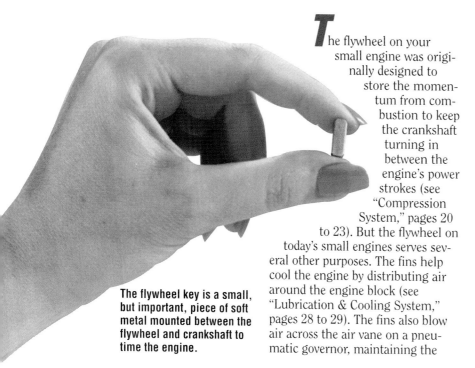

The flywheel key is a small, but important, piece of soft metal mounted between the flywheel and crankshaft to time the engine.

*T*he flywheel on your small engine was originally designed to store the momentum from combustion to keep the crankshaft turning in between the engine's power strokes (see "Compression System," pages 20 to 23). But the flywheel on today's small engines serves several other purposes. The fins help cool the engine by distributing air around the engine block (see "Lubrication & Cooling System," pages 28 to 29). The fins also blow air across the air vane on a pneumatic governor, maintaining the desired engine speed (see "Governor System," pages 30 to 31). Magnets mounted in the outside surface of the flywheel are required for ignition (see "Ignition System," pages 26 to 27). On engines with starter motors, lights or other devices, magnets mounted inside and outside the flywheel are at the heart of the electrical system (see "Electrical System," pages 34 to 35).

Finally, if a lawn mower or tiller blade hits a rock or curb, the flywheel key (left) can sometimes absorb the damage, reducing repair costs significantly. Always check for damage by removing the flywheel to inspect the key and the keyway, the key's slot on the crankshaft. The soft metal key must eliminate play between the flywheel and crankshaft.

Removing the flywheel

1. Disconnect the spark plug lead and secure it away from the spark plug. Then, loosen the bolts holding the shroud in place and remove the shroud.

2. If the engine is equipped with a flywheel brake, remove any cover and disconnect the outer end of the brake spring (photo A).

3. If the flywheel is equipped with a flywheel clutch, remove it with a flywheel clutch tool while holding the flywheel with a flywheel holder or a flywheel strap wrench (see "Specialty Tools," page 130). If the flywheel is attached with a nut, use the flywheel holder as a brace, and remove the flywheel retaining nut with the appropriate socket (photo B).

4. With the flywheel nut threaded onto the crankshaft, install a flywheel puller so its bolts engage the holes adjacent to the flywheel's hub (photo C). If the holes are not threaded, use a self-tapping flywheel puller or tap the holes using a ¼ × 20 tap. CAUTION: Never strike the flywheel. Even a slightly damaged flywheel presents a safety hazard and must be replaced.

5. Rotate the puller nuts evenly until the flywheel pops free. Then, remove the flywheel and key.

Inspecting the flywheel and key

1. Check for cracks on your crankshaft or broken fins on the flywheel. Replace them if you find such damage. The tapered sections must be clean and smooth, with no play between the two.

2. Inspect the keyway and flywheel (photo D) for damage. Slight burrs may be removed with a file. Then, make certain there is no play or wobbling when the flywheel is placed on the crankshaft.

3. Inspect the flywheel key. If there are any signs of shearing or if you have doubts about the condition of your flywheel key, replace it. It's simple and inexpensive.

Installing the flywheel

First, obtain a new flywheel key designed for your make and model from your authorized service dealer.

1. Place the flywheel on the crankshaft and look through the flywheel hub to align the keyways on the flywheel and crankshaft.

2. With the flywheel in place, place the key in the keyway; it should fit securely. If you feel play, check to see if the key is upside down. Debris can also prevent the key from seating in the keyway.

3. Once the key and flywheel are securely in place, reattach the flywheel nut or clutch. Consult your authorized service dealer for the torque specifications for your make and model.

A

B

C

Crankshaft keyways

D

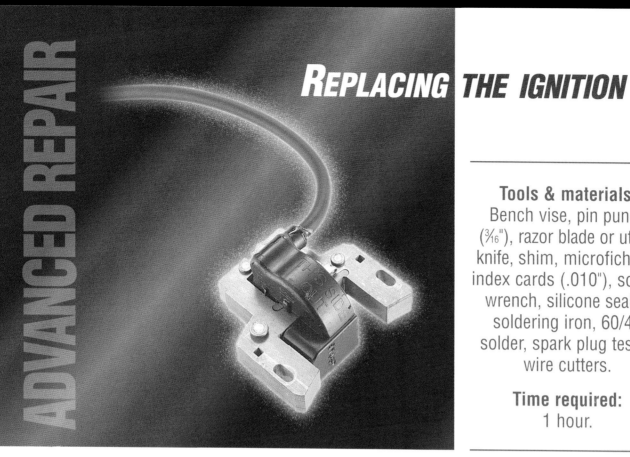

REPLACING *THE IGNITION*

Tools & materials:
Bench vise, pin punch (³⁄₁₆"), razor blade or utility knife, shim, microfiche or index cards (.010"), socket wrench, silicone sealer, soldering iron, 60/40 solder, spark plug tester, wire cutters.

Time required:
1 hour.

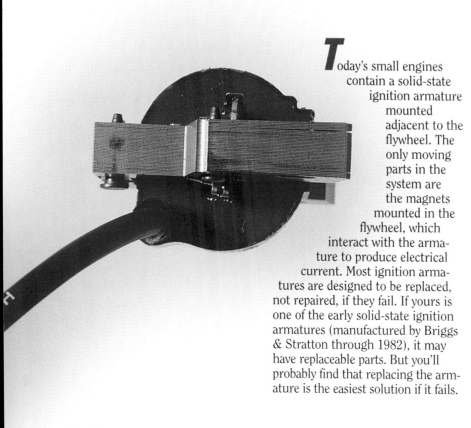

*T*oday's small engines contain a solid-state ignition armature mounted adjacent to the flywheel. The only moving parts in the system are the magnets mounted in the flywheel, which interact with the armature to produce electrical current. Most ignition armatures are designed to be replaced, not repaired, if they fail. If yours is one of the early solid-state ignition armatures (manufactured by Briggs & Stratton through 1982), it may have replaceable parts. But you'll probably find that replacing the armature is the easiest solution if it fails.

Most engines built through the early 1980s contain a set of mechanical points, known as breaker points, under the flywheel. The points open and close an electrical circuit required for ignition. You can improve the reliability of such an engine, if it's a Briggs & Stratton, by bypassing the breaker points system using a solid-state ignition retrofit kit. It's an easy modification. Before you replace a suspect ignition armature, always test ignition with a spark tester (see "Servicing Spark Plugs," pages 50 to 51). Check for faulty electrical switches that could be the source of the problem (see "Braking System," page 32). This section covers the procedures for replacing the ignition armature and bypassing a breaker points system with a solid-state system.

Installing and adjusting a new ignition armature

An ignition armature must be set at a precise distance from the flywheel. Ask your authorized service dealer for the proper gap for your engine. Common armature gap ranges are .006-.010" and .010-.014". Armatures are often packaged with a shim to assist in setting the gap. Microfiche or index cards of the proper thickness also work well.

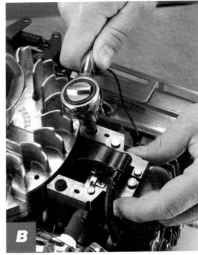

1. Remove the old ignition armature mounting screws (photo A). Then, disconnect the stop switch wire from the flywheel brake (see "Removing a Brake Pad," page 123) and remove the armature.

2. Attach a replacement armature from the original engine manufacturer, using mounting screws (photo A). Then, push the armature away from the flywheel and tighten one screw (photo B).

3. Turn the flywheel so the magnets are on the opposite side from the ignition armature (photo C).

4. Place the appropriate shim between the rim of the flywheel and the ignition armature. While holding the shim, turn the flywheel until the magnets are directly adjacent to the armature (photo D).

5. Loosen the tight screw so the magnets pull the ignition armature against the flywheel and shim. Then, tighten both mounting screws and rotate the flywheel until the shim slips free.

Testing a stop switch

1. Insert the spark plug lead on one end of a spark tester and attach the tester's alligator clip to ground, such as an engine bolt (photo E).

2. Place the equipment stop switch control in the OFF or STOP position. If the engine is not connected to the equipment, ground the stop switch wire to the cylinder. Attempt to start the engine using the rewind cord or key (if equipped). There should be no spark. If a spark appears, inspect the stop switch for damage. Consult your authorized service dealer if you find a faulty switch.

3. Place the stop switch control in the RUN or START position. If the engine is not connected to the equipment, make sure the stop switch wire is not

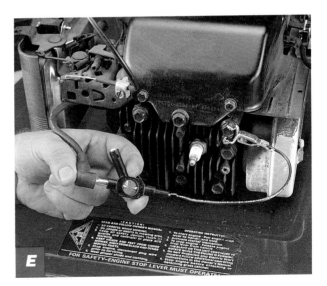

grounded. Attempt to start the engine. A spark should be visible in the tester. If no spark appears, check for broken wires, shorts, grounds or a defective stop switch.

4. Once you have confirmed that the stop switch is working, reconnect the spark plug lead.

The evolution of the ignition armature

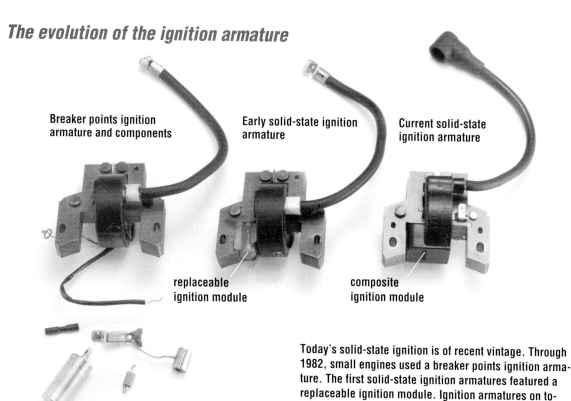

Breaker points ignition armature and components

Early solid-state ignition armature

Current solid-state ignition armature

replaceable ignition module

composite ignition module

Today's solid-state ignition is of recent vintage. Through 1982, small engines used a breaker points ignition armature. The first solid-state ignition armatures featured a replaceable ignition module. Ignition armatures on today's small engines contain a composite ignition module.

Retrofitting an older ignition armature

Breaker point ignition systems were common through 1982. You can improve ignition reliability on a single-cylinder Briggs & Stratton engine equipped with breaker points and a two-leg armature by installing a solid-state ignition conversion kit that bypasses the points. Consult an authorized service dealer for the proper conversion kit.

1. Disconnect the spark plug lead and secure it away from the plug. Then, remove the flywheel and discard the old flywheel key.

2. Cut the armature primary and stop switch wires as close as possible to the dust cover (photo A). Then, remove the dust cover, points and plunger, and plug the plunger hole with the plug supplied in the conversion kit.

3. Loosen the screws and remove the armature. Then, cut the armature's primary wire to a 3" length (photo B). Strip away ⅝" of the outer insulation. Then, use a utility knife or razor blade to scrape off thoroughly the red varnish insulation underneath. Take care not to nick or cut the wire (photo C).

4. Install the conversion module (photo D). Modify the air vane brackets or guides for clearance, as required.

5. Fasten a pin punch in a bench vise. Push open the spring-loaded wire retainer by pressing down on the punch. With the slot open, insert the armature's primary wire and a new stop switch wire (if required), together with the module primary wire (photo E). Then, release the wire re-

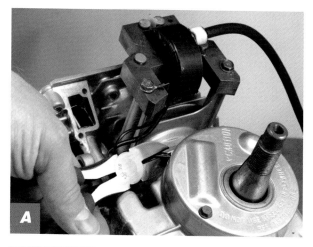

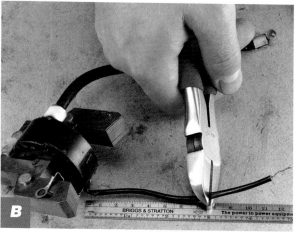

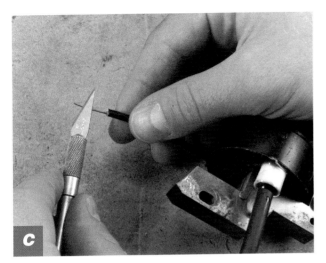

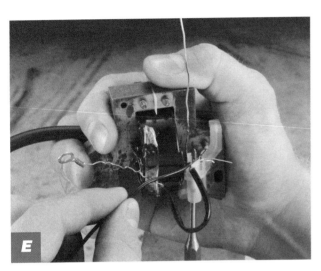

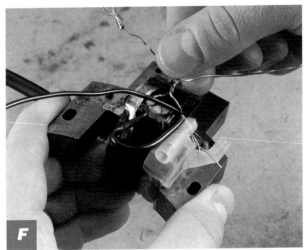

tainer, locking the wires in place. Secure the wires by soldering the ends with 60/40 rosin core solder.

6. Twist the armature ground wire and module ground wire together (two turns) close to the armature coil (photo F) and solder the twisted section, taking care not to damage the armature coil casing. Avoid crossing these wires with those inserted in the wire retainer in Step 5.

7. Remove the shortest ground wire by cutting it off close to the soldered connection. Cement the wires to the armature coil, using a generous amount of silicon sealer to protect against vibrations.

8. Use a screw to attach the armature/module ground wire to the armature (photo G). Then, fasten the armature to the engine so that the wire retainer is toward the cylinder.

9. Remove the remainder of the original stop switch wire as close as possible to the terminal on the engine. Then, route the new wire from the module, following the same path as the original. Fasten the new wire in place. Make sure the wire does not interfere with the flywheel.

10. Install the flywheel, using the replacement flywheel key in your kit, and tighten the flywheel nut or rewind clutch (see "Inspecting the Flywheel & Key," pages 98 to 99). Set the armature air gap (see "Installing and Adjusting a New Ignition Armature," page 101). Then, test the stop switches (see "Testing a Stop Switch," page 101).

TESTING THE ELECTRICAL SYSTEM

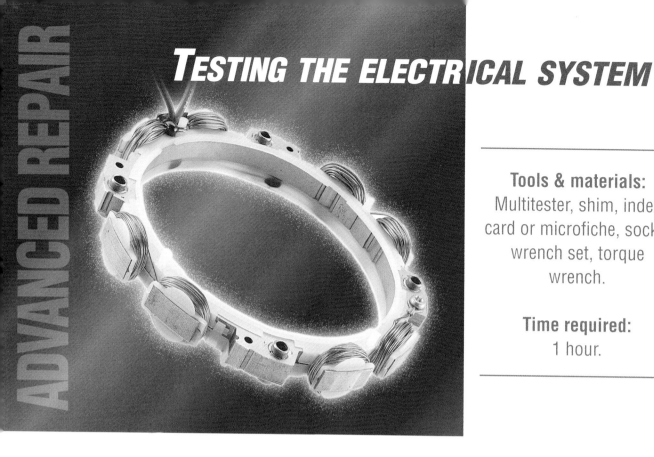

Tools & materials:
Multitester, shim, index card or microfiche, socket wrench set, torque wrench.

Time required:
1 hour.

Small engines that start with a key require an electrical system to charge the battery and to power on-board electrical devices. If you hear a groan or just a click when you try to start a small engine equipped with an electric starter motor, your electrical system may be the source of the problem. Electrical problems can also keep on-board electrical devices from operating. The proper test can help you identify the source of the problem.

When testing an alternator or other electrical system component, use the chart (right) to determine the correct test. The chart includes the most common electrical systems on Briggs & Stratton engines and illustrates the proper way to attach a multitester to your engine. If you own an engine produced by another manufacturer, ask your authorized service dealer how to connect the alternator for testing.

This section also explains how to replace your stator, if necessary. On most models, the stator is mounted under the flywheel and is not difficult to replace once the flywheel is removed. On some walk-behind lawn mowers, the stator is mounted outside the flywheel, making replacement even simpler.

Selecting the right test for your alternator

1. With the engine off, locate the thin wire(s) extending from beneath the blower housing. These wires attach to the stator under the flywheel and deliver the electrical current from the stator to the battery and other electrical devices.

2. Note the color of the wires (scrape away any engine paint to identify the true wire color), as well as the color of the wire connector, typically an inch or two from the blower housing. For a Briggs & Stratton engine, find the same wire/connector combination on the chart (right). The chart tells you the type of test to perform (AC Volts or DC Amps), how to set your multitester leads and the correct engine test speed and multitester readings.

3. Use the appropriate test procedure on page 106. If the wiring on your engine is not on the chart, ask your authorized service dealer how to test your equipment.

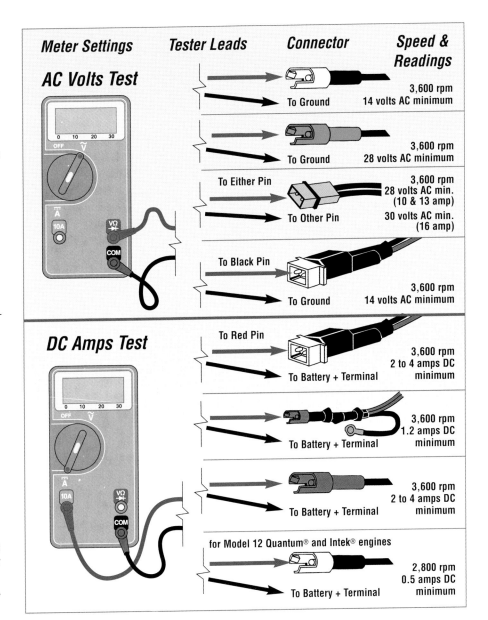

Meter Settings	Tester Leads	Connector	Speed & Readings
AC Volts Test		To Ground	3,600 rpm 14 volts AC minimum
		To Ground	3,600 rpm 28 volts AC minimum
	To Either Pin / To Other Pin		3,600 rpm 28 volts AC min. (10 & 13 amp) / 30 volts AC min. (16 amp)
	To Black Pin / To Ground		3,600 rpm 14 volts AC minimum
DC Amps Test	To Red Pin / To Battery + Terminal		3,600 rpm 2 to 4 amps DC minimum
	To Battery + Terminal		3,600 rpm 1.2 amps DC minimum
	To Battery + Terminal		3,600 rpm 2 to 4 amps DC minimum
	for Model 12 Quantum® and Intek® engines		
	To Battery + Terminal		2,800 rpm 0.5 amps DC minimum

BATTERY SAFETY

Small engines typically use lead-acid batteries, which store electrical energy using lead plates and sulfuric acid. The electrolyte fluid in the battery loses its sulfuric acid and gains water as the battery is discharged.

Battery electrolyte is extremely corrosive and can cause severe burns to eyes and skin. Batteries produce hydrogen gas that can cause an explosion if ignited by a spark or open flame. Minimize safety hazards by observing these precautions.

• Follow the manufacturer's recommended procedure for charging, installation, removal and disposal.
• ALWAYS hold a battery upright to avoid spilling electrolyte.
• Wear protective eyewear and clothing when handling batteries.
• If electrolyte spills on skin or splashes in an eye, flush immediately with lots of cold water and contact a physician immediately.
• Service batteries in a well-ventilated area, away from sources of sparks or flames.

Conducting an AC VOLTS test

If your engine requires an AC VOLTS test (see chart, page 105), set the tester's dial to AC VOLTS and follow these steps:

1. Insert the black multitester lead into the tester's COM receptacle. Connect the other end to ground, such as an engine bolt or cylinder fin, or to the double connector on the stator output wires.

2. Insert the red lead on the multitester into the tester's AC VOLTS receptacle. Connect the red lead to the appropriate stator output wire (photo A).

3. Start the engine and let it run for several minutes to reach its operating temperature. Then, using a tachometer, set the engine test speed and check the reading on the tester. Replace the stator if the reading is incorrect (see chart, page 105).

4. Turn off the engine and disconnect the multitester from your equipment.

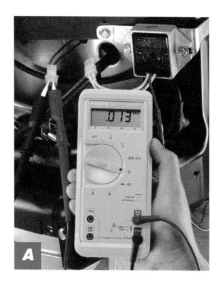

Conducting a DC AMPS test

If your engine requires a DC AMPS test (see chart, page 105), set the tester's dial to DC AMPS and follow these steps:

1. Insert the black multitester lead into the tester's COM receptacle. Connect the other end to the battery's positive terminal. (NOTE: The battery must be grounded to the equipment frame or the engine block to create a complete circuit.)

2. Insert the red lead on the multitester into the tester's AMPS receptacle. Connect the red lead to the appropriate stator output wire (see chart, page 105) (photo B).

3. Start the engine and let it run for several minutes to reach its operating temperature. Then, using a tachometer, set the engine test speed and check the reading on the multitester. An incorrect reading indicates that the stator, diode or regulator should be replaced.

4. Turn off the engine and disconnect the tester from your equipment.

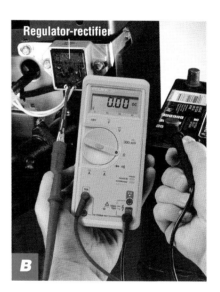

Replacing a stator under the flywheel

In most cases, you need to remove the blower housing, rotating screen, rewind clutch and flywheel to get to the stator (see "Inspecting the Flywheel & Key," pages 98 to 99). If your stator is mounted outside the flywheel, follow the instructions under "Replacing an External Stator" (opposite).

1. With the flywheel removed, note the path of the stator wires, under one coil spool and between the starter and starter drive housing.

2. Remove the ground wire or rectifier assembly (if equipped) from the starter drive housing. Then, remove the stator mounting screws and bushings.

3. Before installing a new stator, locate the stator wires against the cylinder and make sure the wires remain clear of the flywheel (photo C).

4. Install a new stator assembly, making certain the output wires are properly positioned. While tightening the mounting screws, push the stator toward the crankshaft to take up clearance in the bushing. Then, tighten the screws to 20 in. lbs.

5. Reinstall the flywheel, screen and blower housing. Then, attach the ground wire or rectifier assembly (if equipped) to the drive housing.

Replacing an external stator

1. Disconnect the stator output wire from wires leading to the battery or other electrical devices.

2. Rotate the flywheel until the magnets are positioned away from the stator. Then, loosen the stator mounting bolts and remove the stator from the engine (photo D).

3. With the flywheel magnets positioned away from the stator, install the new stator, leaving a wide gap between the stator and flywheel. Tighten one of the mounting bolts.

4. Reattach the stator output wires. Then, follow the procedure for "Adjusting the Air Gap on an External Stator" (below).

Adjusting the air gap on an external stator

The gap between the stator and the flywheel must be set precisely for the stator to function properly. Many stators require a .010" stator air gap. Consult your authorized service dealer for the proper gap for your stator.

1. Rotate the flywheel until the magnets are positioned away from the stator.

2. Loosen both stator mounting bolts and move the stator away from the flywheel. Then, tighten one of the mounting bolts.

3. Place a shim or microfiche card of the proper thickness between the stator and the flywheel (photo E).

4. Turn the flywheel until the magnets are adjacent to the stator.

5. Loosen the tightened bolt and let the magnets pull the stator until it is flush with the shim.

6. Tighten both mounting bolts to 25 in. lbs. (photo F).

7. Turn the flywheel while pulling on the shim to release it.

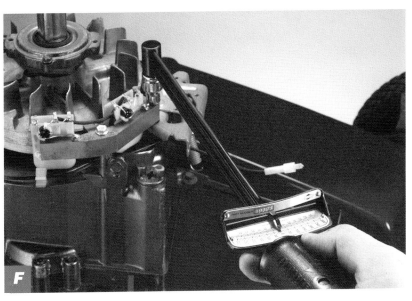

REMOVING CARBON DEPOSITS

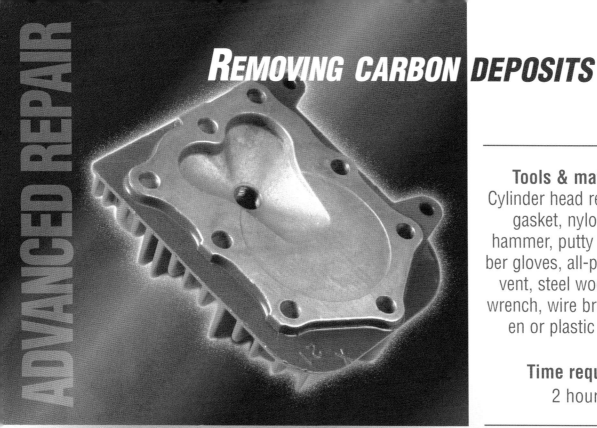

Tools & materials:
Cylinder head replacement gasket, nylon-faced hammer, putty knife, rubber gloves, all-purpose solvent, steel wool, torque wrench, wire brush, wooden or plastic scraper.

Time required:
2 hours.

All rubber components are subject to distortion if carb cleaner is sprayed directly on them.

*O*ne by-product of combustion is carbon, the black soot that can collect and harden on the cylinder head, cylinder wall, piston and valves. Carbon deposits in the combustion chamber can affect engine performance, resulting in higher oil consumption, engine knocking or overheating.

Using unleaded gasoline reduces carbon deposits, but you should still remove the cylinder once each 100 hours of operation and scrape off the carbon, using the tools and solvents described in this section. Clean the cylinder more frequently if you use your engine heavily.

Removing engine components

The first step in servicing the cylinder head is reaching the cylinder head. You may need to remove some other components first.

1. Remove the muffler, muffler guard and any other components that block access to the cylinder.

2. Cylinder head bolts near the muffler and exhaust port may be longer. To avoid confusion, prepare a template. Draw a rough outline of the cylinder head on a piece of cardboard and punch holes for each bolt location. Then, remove the cylinder head bolts and insert them in the corresponding holes.

3. Remove each cylinder head bolt and store it in its respective slot in the cardboard until you are ready to reinstall the cylinder head (photo A).

4. Lift off the cylinder head. If the head sticks, strike it on the side with a nylon-faced hammer. This should loosen the cylinder head enough for you to gently lift it off the engine. NOTE: Do not pry off the cylinder head. This can damage the surface of the engine block or the cylinder head.

5. Remove and discard the old head gasket (photo C).

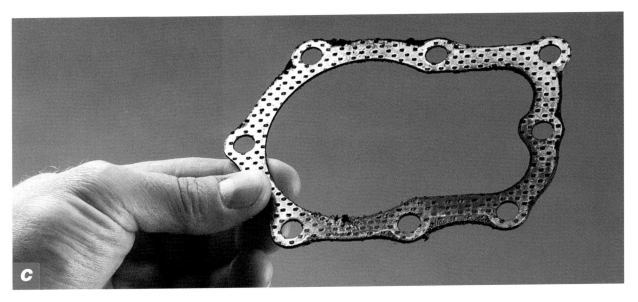

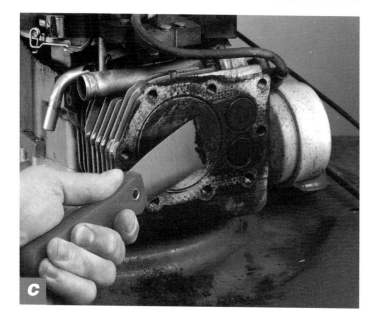

Removing carbon deposits

Always wear protective eyewear and solvent-proof gloves when removing carbon. Ask your authorized service dealer to recommend an all-purpose solvent that will not harm aluminum or plastic components or leave unwanted residues.

1. Place the piston at top dead center so that the valves are closed. Then, scrape carbon gently from the cylinder head, using a wooden or plastic scraper. Take care not to dig the scraper into the aluminum. On stubborn deposits, use a putty knife, wire brush or steel wool (photos A, B and C), taking care not to bear down on the metal surfaces.

2. Clean away the remaining carbon with solvent, using fine steel wool to smooth rough spots. You can also soak metal parts for up to 15 minutes to remove stubborn deposits. Scrape again, if necessary, to loosen stubborn grit. Then, clean the area thoroughly with the solvent and set the head aside.

3. With the piston still at the top of the cylinder and the valves closed, use the same method to remove carbon deposits from the piston and the end of the cylinder (photo C).

4. Turn the crankshaft to open each valve, and carefully remove any visible carbon deposits on the valves and valve seats (photo D), using only a brass wire brush. CAUTION: Do not allow grit to fall into the valve chambers or between the piston and the cylinder wall (photo E).

5. Inspect the valves and valve seats to see if they are cracked, rough or warped. Bring damaged parts to an authorized service dealer for inspection before reassembling the head.

6. Using a scraper, solvent or both, remove any remaining carbon and residue left behind by the head gasket on the cylinder head and engine block. Clean the surfaces thoroughly before installing the new head gasket. Any debris or oil left on the cylinder head or engine block may prevent a tight seal and cause eventual engine damage.

Reassembling the cylinder head

1. Inspect the surfaces of the engine block, cylinder head and new head gasket to be sure they are clean.

2. Place the new head gasket in position on the engine block. Do not use sealing compounds.

3. Set the cylinder head on the head gasket, aligning the cylinder head with the gasket and the engine block.

4. Remove each head bolt from its slot in the cardboard template (photo F). Then, insert the bolt in its original location, leaving it loose. Insert the other bolts in the same fashion. Make sure to attach any housings or brackets that are held in place by the head bolts.

5. Hand-tighten the head bolts first, without using a wrench.

6. Tighten the cylinder head bolts in increments, using a torque wrench. Turn each bolt a few turns, then proceed to the next bolt until each bolt is just snug. For final tightening, use a torque wrench. Proceed in increments of roughly one-third the final torque. Consult your owner's manual for the final torque sequence and specifications. Avoid tightening a single bolt all the way before tightening the other bolts. Uneven tightening is likely to warp the cylinder head.

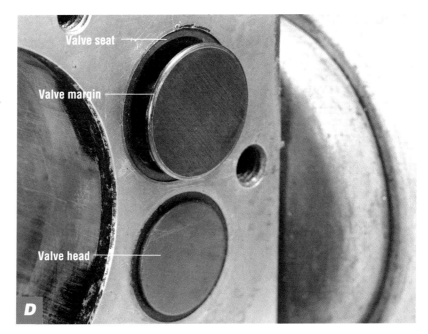

Use solvent to loosen deposits on the valve seats, faces, margins (see illustration, page 113) and heads, and on the cylinder wall and piston head. Then, use a scraper to remove stubborn deposits. Clean the engine block around the cylinder with solvent as well. Inspect the area for grit or debris before attaching a new gasket and the cylinder head.

SERVICING THE VALVES

Tools & materials:
Feeler gauge set, hex wrench set, needlenose pliers, nut driver set, calipers, safety eyewear, socket wrench set, torque wrench, lapping compound, valve lapping tool, valve spring compressor.

Time required:
90 minutes.

A valve spring compressor is an essential tool for removing and installing valves on L-head engines and some overhead valve engines.

*V*alves control the flow of fuel vapor into the combustion chamber and the flow of exhaust gases leaving the engine. Faulty or dirty valves may stick and can develop pits, cracks or grooves that cause the engine to lose power and fuel efficiency.

When you remove the valves from the engine, inspect them carefully. Then, if the valves are not badly worn and the parts are not damaged, you can tune up the valves and seats (see "Lapping the Valves," page 117) so that the valves seal effectively.

Valves contain a *stem, neck, head* and *face.* Each valve stem moves in a *valve guide* that is machined directly in the *cylinder block* or in a replaceable *bushing.* Each valve also moves through a *valve spring,* adjacent to the guide, that pushes the valve toward the closed position and holds the valve face against the valve seat. Each valve spring is held in place by a *valve spring retainer.* Some valve assemblies also include a *rotator,* a circular component that turns the valve slightly in each cycle to ensure a symmetrical wear pattern on valves and seats. Valves are opened by *tappets* that ride on the *camshaft* inside the crankcase.

This section covers the procedures for removing, inspecting, cleaning and replacing valves and related parts.

Valve design

Valve design for the four-stroke small engine includes one intake valve and one exhaust valve per cylinder. The diagrams on this page show the parts of typical valves in detail and their locations in the engine.

Intake valves open to allow the air-fuel mixture to enter the combustion chamber. Exhaust valves open to allow spent fuel gases to leave the engine. Both valves close to seal the combustion chamber for the piston's compression stroke.

Valve springs push the valves toward the closed position, so that they open only at precisely timed intervals. The valves are pushed open by tappets that ride on the *lobes* of the camshaft. The camshaft turns along with the crankshaft; both are driven by the movement of the *piston.* This synchronizes the actions of the valves with those of the piston.

In L-head engines, the valves are located to one side of the cylinder. The valve stems run through the cylinder block, parallel to the piston.

In overhead valve engines, the valves are located in a cylinder head that is much larger than that found in an L-head engine. Overhead valves are pushed open by pivoting rocker arms, operated by *push rods.* The push rods, in turn, are pushed toward the rocker arms by the tappets. The slightly more complex design yields greater power.

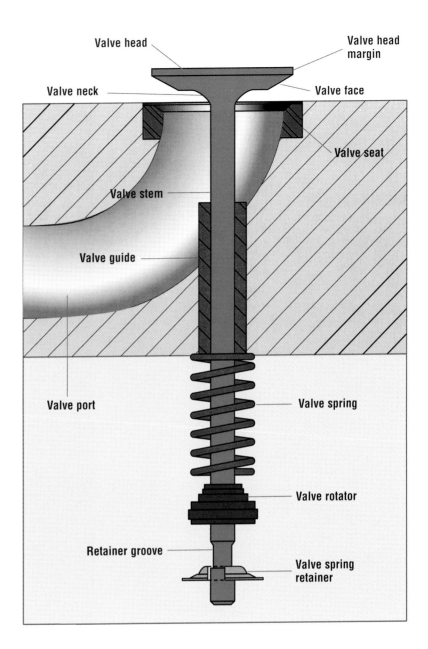

L-head

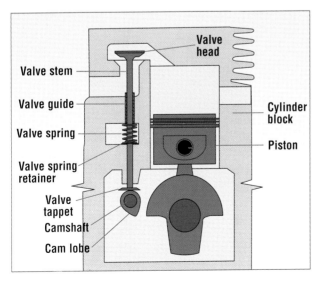

Overhead valve (OHV)

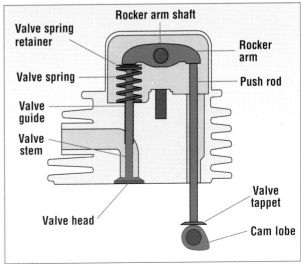

A

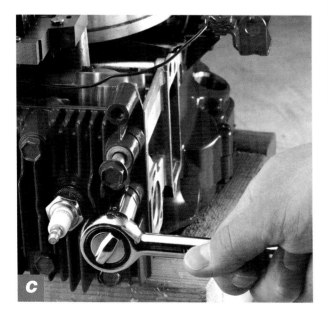

B

C

Reaching the valve chamber

Before you can service the valves, remove engine components that interfere. NOTE: Always wear safety eyewear when removing and installing valves.

1. Remove the muffler (see "Inspecting & Changing the Muffler," pages 62 to 65), crankcase breather (see "Additional Maintenance," pages 56 to 57) and any other components that block access to the valve chamber (photos A and B).

2. Remove the cylinder head bolts (photo C). Label the bolts, if necessary, to ensure proper installation later, since they may be of different lengths (see "Removing Carbon Deposits," pages 108 to 111).

USING A VALVE SPRING COMPRESSOR

If you plan to remove the valves from your engine, a valve spring compressor is a must. Removing valves without this tool is unsafe and can be an exercise in frustration. The method for using the tool varies depending on the type of valve assembly and the design of the engine block. Some valve assemblies hold the valve spring in place with a pin or a pair of collar-shaped automotive-type retainers. Others use a retainer with a keyhole-shaped slot that locks onto the valve stem. No matter which type of retainer you find on your valves, a valve spring compressor allows you to do the job right.

Removing the valves (automotive type or pin retainers)

1. Adjust the jaws of the valve spring compressor until they touch the top and bottom of the valve chamber.

2. Push the tool in until the upper jaw slips over the upper end of the spring. Tighten the jaws to compress the spring (photo D).

3. Remove the retainers and lift out the valves, compressors and springs.

Removing the valves (keyhole retainers)

Removing keyhole retainers requires some patience. Keep in mind the retainer's key-shaped slot. This will help you slip the retainer off the valve stem, even when the retainer is hidden from view by the valve spring compressor.

1. Slip the upper jaw of the valve spring compressor over the top of the valve chamber and the lower jaw between the spring and retainer. If the engine design does not permit the upper jaw to fit over the top of the valve chamber, insert the upper jaw into the chamber over the top of the spring, so that the spring is between the tool's jaws (photo E).

2. Rotate the handle on the valve spring compressor clockwise to compress the spring. Then, slide the retainer off the valve by shifting it with needlenose pliers so that the large part of the keyhole is directly over the stem. Use the pliers to remove the retainer from the valve chamber (photo F).

3. With the valve spring compressor clamping the spring, remove the tool and spring from the chamber. Then, slowly crank open the valve spring compressor to release the tension and remove the spring.

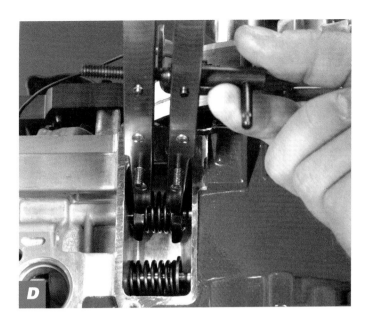

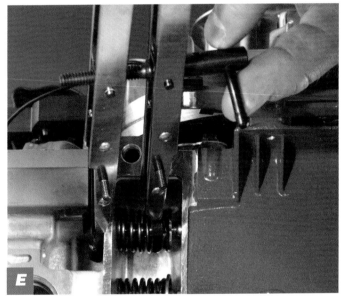

Inspecting the valves

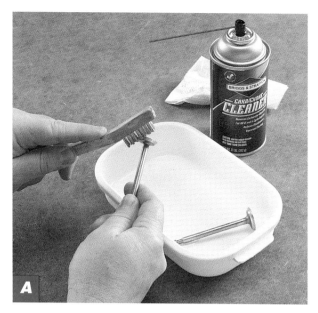

Before wiping or cleaning the valves, look them over carefully. Residue on the valves may help you identify a specific problem. Gummy deposits on the intake valve go hand in hand with a decrease in engine performance, often because the engine has been run on old gasoline. Hard deposits on either valve suggest burning oil, which has several possible causes (see "Troubleshooting," pages 60 to 61). Follow the steps below to check for the most likely sources of valve problems.

1. Check the valve face for an irregular seating pattern. The pattern around the face should be even with the valve head and of equal thickness all the way around. Then, look for stubborn deposits. Remove them with a wire brush and solvent, soaking the parts for several hours, if necessary, to loosen hardened grit (photo A).

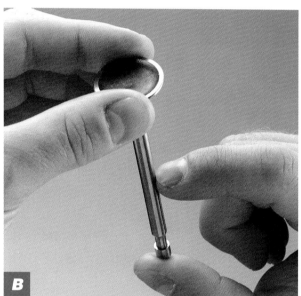

2. Run a fingernail or credit card along the valve stem once you have cleaned it (photo B). If you feel a ridge, the valve stem is worn and should be replaced. Keep in mind that the valve guide may also be worn and need replacement by a machinist (see "Machining Valves," page 114).

3. Measure the thickness of the valve head, known as the valve head margin, using a caliper (photo C). Replace the valve if the margin measures less than ¼".

4. Examine the surfaces of the valve face and seat. An uneven wear pattern tells you it's time to replace them both or resurface the seat and replace the valve (see "Machining Valves," page 114).

5. Check that both valve springs are straight (photo D). Replace either spring if it is bent. NOTE: The exhaust valve spring may use thicker wire than the intake valve spring.

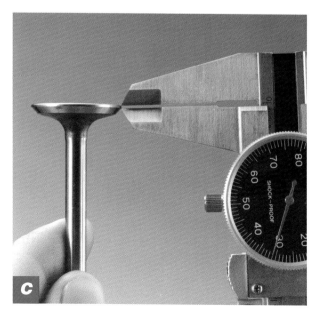

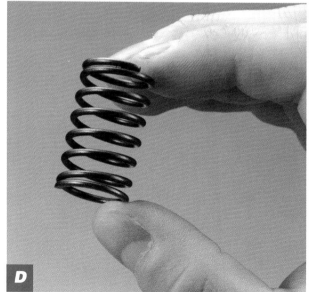

Lapping the valves

You can smooth out minor scoring and pitting of the valve face and seat and restore a valve's ability to seal the combustion chamber by lapping the valves. This procedure involves gently rotating the valve in the seat with a layer of lapping compound—a fine, but abrasive, paste—in between the valve and seat. A lapping tool is used to hold and rotate the valve. During lapping, you'll need to check your progress often. Otherwise, it is easy to remove not only the carbon buildup, but also much of the metal, further damaging the valve or seat.

1. Apply a small amount of valve lapping compound to the valve face and insert the valve into the valve guide.

2. Wet the end of the lapping tool suction cup and place it on the valve head. Spin the valve back and forth between your hands several times. Lift the tool, rotate ¼ turn and spin again (photo E).

3. Clean the surface frequently and check your progress. Lap only enough to create a consistent and even pattern around the valve face.

4. Once lapping is completed, clean the valves thoroughly with solvent to ensure that ALL of the abrasive residue is removed. Any particles that remain can rapidly damage the valves and other engine components.

Adjusting tappet clearances

Since lapping removes a small amount of material from the surfaces of the valve face and valve seat, you may need to adjust the tappet clearances—the spacing between the valve stem and the tappet—after lapping and reinstalling the valves. Ask your authorized service dealer for the correct tappet clearance for your engine.

1. With each valve installed in its proper guides in the cylinder, turn the crankshaft (clockwise as viewed from the flywheel end of the crankshaft) to top dead center. Both valves should be closed. Then, turn the crankshaft past top dead center until the piston is ¼" down from the top of the cylinder.

2. Check the clearance between each valve and its tappet, using a feeler gauge.

3. If clearance is insufficient, remove the valve and grind or file the end of the valve stem square to increase the clearance. Check the length frequently as it is easy to remove too much metal.

4. Once the individual valve parts have been thoroughly cleaned, lubricate the valve stems and guides, using valve guide lubricant. Then, make certain there is NO lubricant on the ends of the valve stems or tappets.

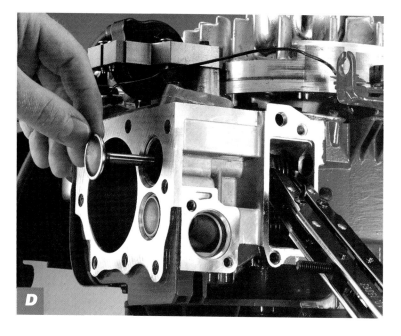

Reinstalling valves with keyhole retainers

You need safety eyewear during this step, to protect yourself from the possibility of a flying spring.

1. Valves with keyhole retainers do not require an additional retainer. Compress the keyhole retainer and spring with the compressor tool—the large hole should face the opening in the tool—until the spring is solid (photo A).

2. Brush the valve stem with valve stem lubricant (photo B).

3. Insert the compressed spring and retainer into the valve chamber (photo C).

4. Insert the valve stem through the large slot in the retainer (photo D). Then, push down and in on the valve compressor until the retainer bottoms out on the valve stem shoulder.

5. Reinstall the crankcase breather and other components.

Installing valves with pins or automotive-type retainers

Once again, safety eyewear is absolutely necessary. Remember: a spring that is under tension can pop loose and fly through the air.

1. Place the valve spring into the valve spring compressor and rotate the tool's handle until the spring is fully compressed.

2. Insert the compressed spring into the valve chamber.

3. Brush the valve stem with valve stem lubricant (photo B). Then, lower the valve stem through the spring (photo D). Hold the spring toward the top of the chamber and the valve in the closed position.

4. If pins are used, insert each pin with needlenose pliers. If automotive-type retainers are used, place the retainers in the valve stem groove.

5. Lower the spring until the retainer fits around the pin or automotive-type retainer. Then, pull out the valve spring compressor.

6. Reinstall the crankcase breather and other components.

Removing overhead valves

Overhead valve designs vary from one engine model to another. The parts and servicing steps in your overhead valve cylinder may differ from the approach that follows, which is based on the Briggs & Stratton Intek® 6-HP single-cylinder OHV. The Intek does not require the use of a valve spring compressor, making valve removal and installation simple.

1. Remove the air cleaner assembly, fuel tank, oil fill tube, blower housing and rewind starter, muffler guard, muffler, carburetor and any other parts that block access to the cylinder head.

2. Remove the screws from the valve cover, using a socket wrench

or nut driver (photo E). Then, remove the valve cover, breather valve assembly (if equipped) and any gaskets.

3. Remove the rocker arm bolts with a socket wrench or nut driver (photo F). Then remove the rocker arms and push rods.

4. Remove the valve caps (if equipped). They are seated on the valve stems (photo G).

5. Use your thumbs to press in on the spring retainer and valve spring over one of the valves. With the valve spring compressed, remove the retainer (photo H).

If your engine uses a keyhole retainer, line up the large slot in the retainer with the valve stem and release the spring slowly so that the

stem slips through the large slot. Then, repeat the procedure for the other valve.

6. Remove the push rod guide bolts and push rod guide.

7. Remove the cylinder head bolts and remove the cylinder head by rocking it with your hands. If necessary, loosen the cylinder head by striking it with a nylon-faced hammer. Never pry it loose, as this may damage the head.

8. Remove and inspect the valves, guides and seats (see "Inspecting the Valves," page 116). The intake and exhaust valves often are made of different steel alloys and may be different colors.

Push rod guide

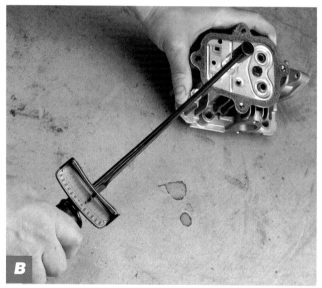

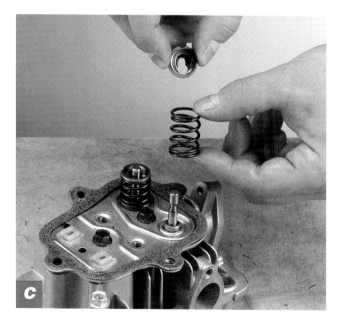

Installing overhead valves

1. Check that valve stems and guides are free of debris and burrs. Then, lightly coat the valve stems with valve guide lubricant and insert them in the cylinder head, taking care to place the correct valve in each valve guide (photo A).

2. Place the push rod guide on the cylinder head and attach the mounting bolts, using a torque wrench (photo B). Coat the rocker arm stud threads with a hardening sealant and install the rocker arm studs, using a socket wrench. Consult your authorized service dealer for the proper torque settings for the mounting bolts and studs.

3. Lubricate the inside diameter of each valve stem seal (if equipped) with engine oil and install the seals on the valve stems. Press them into place.

4. Install a valve spring and retainer over each stem (photo C). Use both thumbs to compress the spring until the valve stem extends through the large end of the key-hole slot. Check that the retainer is fully engaged in the valve stem groove. Repeat this step for the other valve.

5. Coat the threads of the cylinder head bolts with valve guide lubricant. Install a new cylinder head gasket on the cylinder, insert the bolts in the cylinder and position the cylinder head on the cylinder.

6. Tighten the cylinder head bolts in increments, using a torque wrench (photo D). Turn each bolt a few turns, then proceed to the next bolt until each bolt is just snug. Then, for final tightening, proceed in increments of roughly one-third the final torque. Consult your owner's manual for final torque specifications. Uneven tightening is likely to warp the cylinder head.

7. Install the push rods through the push rod guides and into the tappets.

8. Install the caps on the ends of the valves and wipe away any lubricant. Then, install the rocker arm assemblies while holding the rocker arms against the valve cap and push rod (photo E).

9. Rotate the flywheel at least two revolutions to be sure the push rods operate the rocker arms.

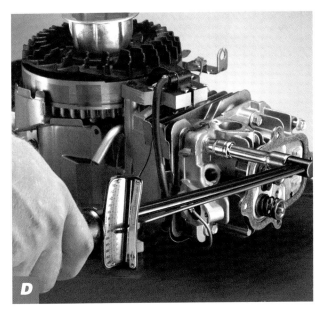

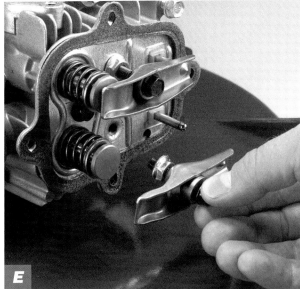

Adjusting overhead valves

1. Release the brake spring. Then, turn the flywheel to close both valves.

2. Insert a narrow screwdriver into the spark plug hole and touch the piston. Turn the flywheel clockwise past top dead center until the piston has moved down ¼". Use the screwdriver to gauge the piston's range of motion (photo F).

3. Check the valve clearance by placing a feeler gauge between the valve head and the rocker arm (photo G). Clearances differ for the two valves and typically range from .002-.004" to .005-.007". Ask your authorized service dealer for the proper valve clearances for your make and model.

4. Adjust the clearances as required by turning the rocker screw. Once adjustments are completed, tighten the rocker nut.

5. Install the valve cover, using new gaskets, as required, and make sure the cover is secure.

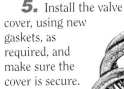

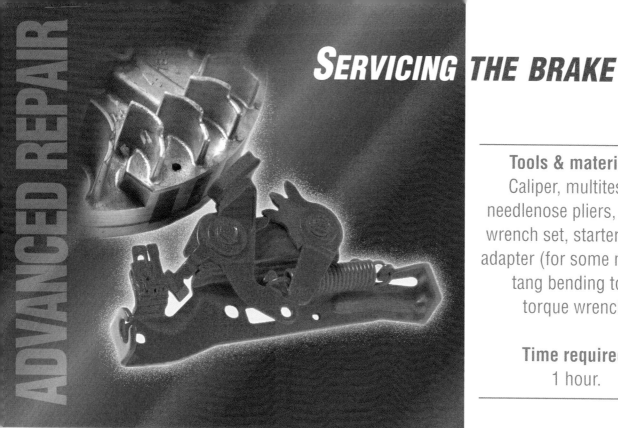

SERVICING THE BRAKE

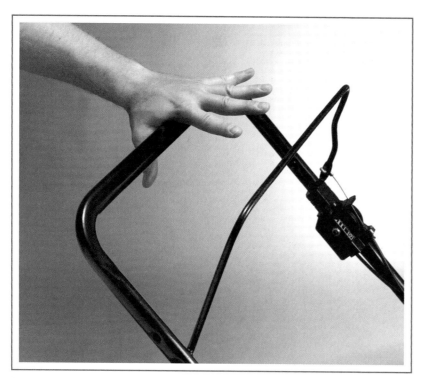

Most small engine equipment is equipped with a brake bail for your safety. The brake bail is designed to protect you by stopping the engine and any cutting equipment any time you release it.

A well-maintained braking system should stop the engine and any attached cutting equipment within three seconds whenever you step away from the equipment or release the brake bail. A brake bail is standard equipment on today's mowers, tillers and other walk-behind equipment. The stop switch immediately grounds the ignition, shutting off the engine, while a brake pad or band stops the flywheel from spinning.

If the engine operates for more than three seconds after the bail is released, the stop switch may be faulty. If the blade spins for more than three seconds, the brake pad or band may be worn or in need of adjustment.

Current models use a brake pad that requires no adjustment. Some older models use a brake band, which may require adjustment by an authorized service technician. This section covers the replacement procedures for the brake band and pad styles.

Removing a brake pad

1. Remove the spark plug lead and secure it away from the spark plug. Then, remove any other components that block access to the brake, such as the finger guard, fuel tank, oil fill tube (photo A), blower housing or rewind starter (photo B).

2. Remove the brake control bracket cover (photo C), if equipped. Then, loosen the cable clamp screw and remove the brake cable from the control lever.

3. Disconnect the spring from the brake anchor, using needlenose pliers (photo D). Then, remove the stop switch wire from the stop switch by gently squeezing the switch and pulling lightly on the wire until it slips free. If the engine is equipped with an electric starter motor, disconnect the pair of wires leading to the starter motor.

4. Loosen the brake bracket screws and remove the bracket from the brake assembly.

A

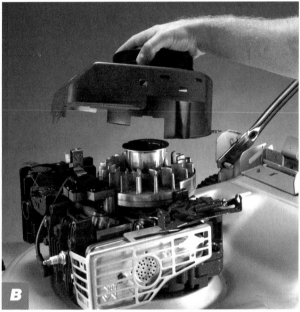

B

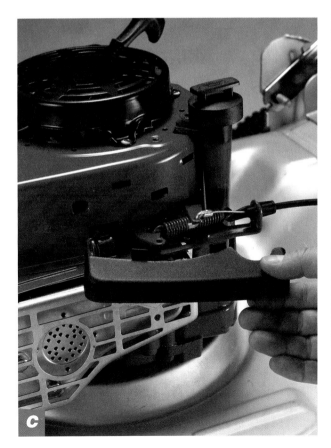

C

D

Inspecting and testing a brake pad system

1. Inspect the brake pad for nicks, cuts, debris and other damage. Check for wear, by measuring the pad's thickness with a ruler or caliper (photo A). NOTE: Measure the pad only, not the bracket. Replace the brake assembly if the pad's thickness is less than .090".

2. Test the stop switch, using a multitester or ohmmeter, to determine whether the ignition circuit is grounded when the stop switch is activated (photo B). The stop switch should show continuity (0 ohms) to engine ground when the switch is set to STOP, and no continuity (∞), when the switch is set to RUN. If you identify a problem, check for loose or faulty connections.

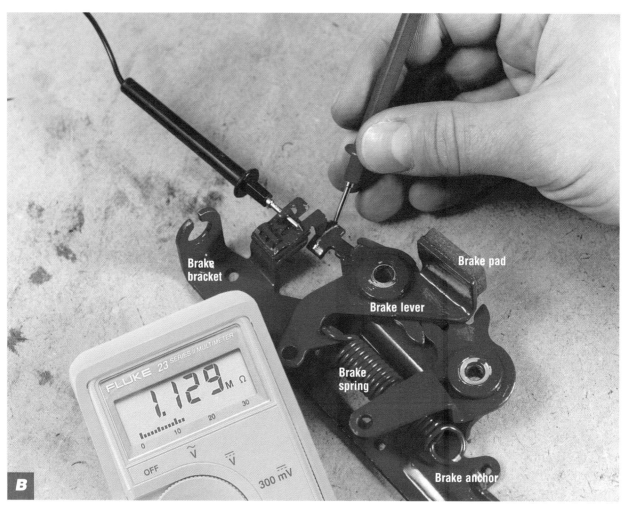

Brake bracket

Brake pad

Brake lever

Brake spring

Brake anchor

Reassembling the braking system

1. Install the brake assembly on the cylinder (photo C). Tighten the mounting bolts to 40 in. lbs., using a torque wrench.

2. Install the stop switch wire, bending the end of the wire 90° (photo D).

3. Install the blower housing and any other engine components removed for brake servicing.

4. Check the braking action by pivoting the lever. Make sure the lever moves freely and the pad makes full contact with the flywheel.

C

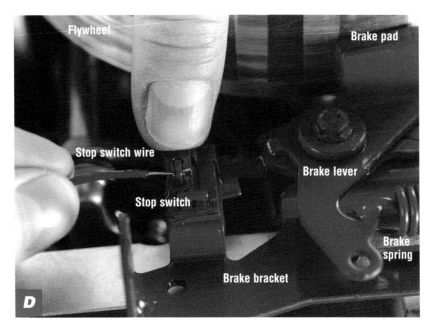

Flywheel
Brake pad
Stop switch wire
Stop switch
Brake lever
Brake bracket
Brake spring

D

5. Attach the brake spring, using needlenose pliers, and connect the brake cable that connects to the brake bail on your walk-behind equipment.

6. Test the braking system by starting the engine and then releasing the brake bail (see photo, below). The engine and the blade or other equipment should come to a stop within three seconds. If you are uncertain about the effectiveness of your braking system, bring the equipment to your authorized service dealer for further inspection.

BRAKE SAFETY

The only safe way to use the brake bail on your small engine equipment is to pull and hold the bail by hand when starting and running the engine. You can release it when necessary to stop the engine. Keeping the bail in the operating position by any other means overrides an important safety mechanism. The bail is required by law and is designed to protect you from injury.

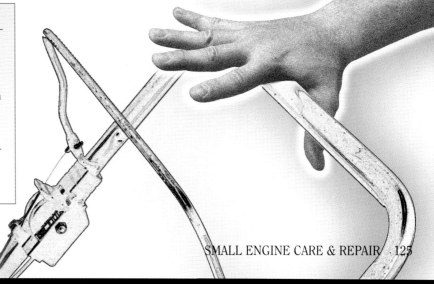

Control lever tang
Band brake loop
Band brake

A

Removing and inspecting a band brake

The brake band contains loops at either end, mounted on a stationary and a movable post. A tang over the movable post prevents the brake band from dislodging during operation.

1. Use a tang bending tool (see "Tang Bending and Other Adjustment Methods," page 84) to bend the control lever tang outward so it clears the band brake loop (photo A).

2. Release the brake spring, using pliers (photo B).

3. Lift the band off the stationary and movable posts (photo C).

4. Inspect the band for damage. Replace it if you find nicks or cuts.

5. Check for wear, by measuring the pad's thickness with a ruler or caliper (photo D). NOTE: Measure the pad only, not the metal band. Replace the brake band if the pad's thickness is less than .030" (photo D).

Brake spring

B

Movable post

C

Testing a band brake

Test the band brake's stopping power with the spark plug lead secured away from the spark plug. On electric start engines, disconnect and remove the battery.

1. With the brake engaged, turn the starter clutch, using a starter clutch adapter and torque wrench (photo E). Turning the flywheel clockwise at a steady rate should require at least 45 in. lbs. of torque. If the torque reading is lower, components may be worn, damaged or in need of adjustment.

2. Test the stop switch, using a multitester or ohmmeter, to determine whether the ignition circuit is grounded when the stop switch is activated. The stop switch should show continuity (0 ohms) to engine

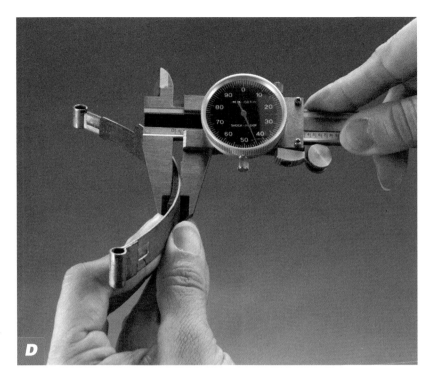

ground when the switch is set to STOP, and no continuity (∞) when the switch is set to RUN. If you discover a problem, check for loose or faulty connections.

Assembling a band brake

1. Reinstall the stop switch wire on the control bracket. On older systems, reinstall the stop switch wire on the control bracket stop switch terminal.

2. Place the band brake on the stationary post and hook it over the end of the movable post until the band bottoms out. NOTE: The brake material on a steel band must be on the flywheel side after assembly. On older systems, install the band brake on the stationary and movable posts.

3. Bend the retainer tang until it is positioned over the band brake loop so that the loop cannot be accidentally dislodged. After assembly, check that the braking material on the metal band faces the flywheel.

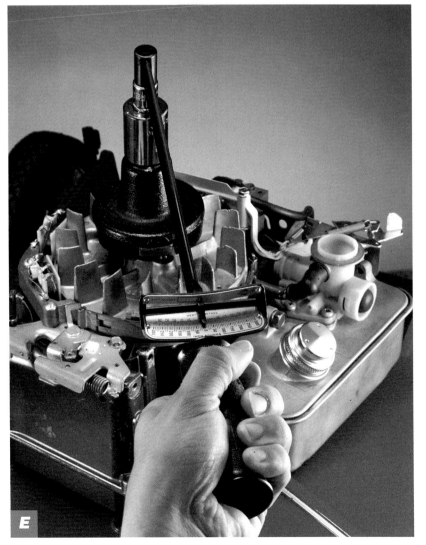

ADDITIONAL TOOLS, PARTS & SUPPLIES

*E*very repair and maintenance procedure in this book is simpler, safer and easier when you use high-quality tools, parts and supplies. Compensating for equipment that isn't up to the task will increase the amount of time and effort you spend, and your repairs will become more frustrating than necessary.

Your tool kit should include the basic hand tools required for small engine maintenance and repairs (see "Maintenance," pages 42 to 57, and "Basic Repair," pages 58-87). If you don't have confidence in your tools, you should replace them. If the ones you have are well made and you keep them in good condition, they'll give

you reliable service for many years.

If you plan to undertake some advanced repair projects, you should also own some specialty tools designed for working with small engines. Review the instructions for each task you expect to handle, and find out if you will need any tools you don't already own.

Although you may be able to borrow some tools from friends or neighbors, be sure to own the tools you'll need most. And if you're not sure whether you should buy a particular tool, remember: it's better to have a tool you don't need than to need a tool you don't have.

At the same time, don't buy a

whole shop full of tools you aren't likely to use or that do much more than you need.

Of course, the cost of specialty tools can strain your repair budget. But once you have learned the procedures in this book, you'll find that investing in new tools is definitely money well spent.

To choose the right tools, ask your authorized service technician for advice, and decide how serious you are about doing your own maintenance and repair work. Then stock your tool bench.

The price of quality tools may be higher, but your satisfaction will be higher too.

Original parts

In addition to using high-quality tools and following instructions carefully, use original engine manufacturer's replacement parts available from authorized service dealers and outdoor power equipment retailers. For more information on how to locate dealers near you, see "Where to Find Us," page 5. Quality replacement parts will make a significant difference in how well your engine performs after a repair.

If parts that meet original equipment manufacturer specifications cost a bit more than others, you'll do well to spend the few extra dollars. Few things are more frustrating than doing everything right and having a job fail because of a faulty part. Your repairs will also stand the test of time with original engine manufacturer's replacement parts. These parts are designed to last a long time.

When you shop for replacement parts, take along your engine model number and a list of the parts you need. You'll save time and avoid repeat trips to the dealer.

Also take along any parts you have removed from your engine. They often help an authorized service dealer identify the right parts for your make and model.

Some of the most common replacement parts for small engines are pictured above. They include:

(A) Air cleaner
(B) Starter rope and grip
(C) Muffler
(D) Carburetors
(E) Spark plug
(F) Oil filter
(G) Valve
(H) Fuel filter
(I) Valve retainer
(J) Piston rings
(K) Piston
(L) Connecting rod

Specialty tools

Tools you may want to purchase to simplify advanced projects include:

(A) Cylinder leakdown tester: for testing sealing capabilities of compression components

(B) Piston ring compressor: for compressing rings during assembly

(C) Starter clutch wrench: for removing and torquing rewind starter clutch

(D) Valve lapping tool: for resurfacing valve faces and seats

(E) Leakdown tester clamp

(F) Plug gauge: for checking valve guides for wear

(G) Telescoping gauge: for measuring inside diameters of cylinders

(H) Brake adjustment gauge: for setting band brakes

(I) C-ring installation tool: for installing a starter motor c-ring

(J) Piston ring expander: for removing and installing piston rings

(K) Flywheel strap wrench: for removing and installing flywheel

(L) Carburetor jet screwdrivers: for removing and installing carburetor jets

(M) C-ring removal tool: for removing c-ring on starter motor

(N) Torque wrench: for tightening bolts to specified "inch pounds" of torque

(O) DC shunt: for measuring current draw of DC motors and output of regulated alternators

An inexpensive magnetic parts pick-up comes in handy when you drop small metal parts in hard-to-reach areas.

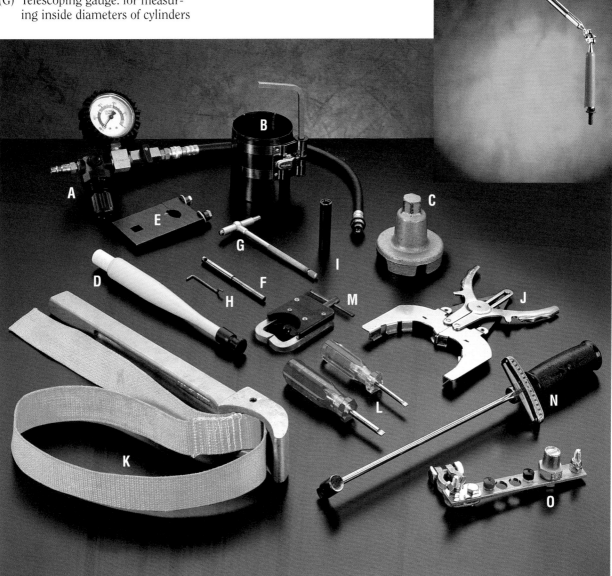

For information concerning the purchase of these tools and supplies, contact Briggs & Stratton Customer Service by phone at 1-800-233-3723, or on the internet at www.briggsandstratton.com

Supplies

To get the best results from your repairs and the highest performance from your small engine, use the lubricants and cleaners recommended by your authorized service dealer or outdoor power equipment retailer. Like tools, cleaners and lubricants are made for specific purposes, and each works best in the physical and chemical environment for which it was intended. Substituting one product for another could prove ineffective, damaging or even dangerous. Your work will be easier and more reliable when you use the right tools, lubricants and cleaners for the job.

The lubricants and cleaners shown above represent the full range of products you need to keep your small engine in peak operating condition. They include:

(A) Moly/graphite grease
(B) White lithium grease
(C) Carburetor/choke cleaner
(D) Fogging oil
(E) Heavy-duty silicone
(F) Battery cleaner
(G) Battery terminal protector
(H) 4-use lubricant
(I) Penetrating oil
(J) Heavy-duty degreaser
(K) Gasoline additive
(L) Valve guide lubricant
(M) Lawn mower oil
(N) Valve lapping compound
(O) Grease gun

Briggs & Stratton publishes a full range of manuals available at authorized service dealers and outdoor power equipment retailers. These books are geared to each engine make and model.

MAINTENANCE LOG FOR:

Date Performed	Maintenance Task	Every 5 Hours	Every 25 Hours or Every Season	Every 50 Hours or Every Season	Every 100 Hours or Every Season	Every 100–300 Hours
	Check Oil Level	X				
	Change Oil*			X		
	Replace Oil-Foam® Element or Optional Pre-cleaner**		X			
	Replace Air-Cleaner Cartridge if No Pre-cleaner**		X			
	Replace Air-Cleaner Cartridge if Equipped with Pre-cleaner**				X	
	Clean Cooling System**				X	
	Inspect Spark-Arrester (If So Equipped)			X		
	Replace In-Line Fuel Filter (Optional Accessory)			X		
	Replace Spark Plug				X	
	Clean Combustion Chamber Deposits					X

* Change oil after first 5 hours of use, then every 50 hours or every season.

**Clean more often under dusty conditions or when airborne debris is present. Replace air-cleaner parts if very dirty.

MISCELLANEOUS NOTES

MAINTENANCE LOG FOR:

Date Performed	Maintenance Task	Every 5 Hours	Every 25 Hours or Every Season	Every 50 Hours or Every Season	Every 100 Hours or Every Season	Every 100–300 Hours
	Check Oil Level	X				
	Change Oil*			X		
	Replace Oil-Foam® Element or Optional Pre-cleaner**		X			
	Replace Air-Cleaner Cartridge if No Pre-cleaner**		X			
	Replace Air-Cleaner Cartridge if Equipped with Pre-cleaner**				X	
	Clean Cooling System**				X	
	Inspect Spark-Arrester (If So Equipped)			X		
	Replace In-Line Fuel Filter (Optional Accessory)			X		
	Replace Spark Plug				X	
	Clean Combustion Chamber Deposits					X

* Change oil after first 5 hours of use, then every 50 hours or every season.

**Clean more often under dusty conditions or when airborne debris is present. Replace air-cleaner parts if very dirty.

MISCELLANEOUS NOTES

MAINTENANCE LOG FOR:

Date Performed	Maintenance Task	Every 5 Hours	Every 25 Hours or Every Season	Every 50 Hours or Every Season	Every 100 Hours or Every Season	Every 100–300 Hours
	Check Oil Level	X				
	Change Oil*			X		
	Replace Oil-Foam® Element or Optional Pre-cleaner**		X			
	Replace Air-Cleaner Cartridge if No Pre-cleaner**		X			
	Replace Air-Cleaner Cartridge if Equipped with Pre-cleaner**				X	
	Clean Cooling System**				X	
	Inspect Spark-Arrester (If So Equipped)			X		
	Replace In-Line Fuel Filter (Optional Accessory)			X		
	Replace Spark Plug				X	
	Clean Combustion Chamber Deposits					X

* Change oil after first 5 hours of use, then every 50 hours or every season.

**Clean more often under dusty conditions or when airborne debris is present. Replace air-cleaner parts if very dirty.

MISCELLANEOUS NOTES

MAINTENANCE LOG FOR:

Date Performed	Maintenance Task	Every 5 Hours	Every 25 Hours or Every Season	Every 50 Hours or Every Season	Every 100 Hours or Every Season	Every 100–300 Hours
	Check Oil Level	X				
	Change Oil*			X		
	Replace Oil-Foam® Element or Optional Pre-cleaner**		X			
	Replace Air-Cleaner Cartridge if No Pre-cleaner**		X			
	Replace Air-Cleaner Cartridge if Equipped with Pre-cleaner**				X	
	Clean Cooling System**				X	
	Inspect Spark-Arrester (If So Equipped)			X		
	Replace In-Line Fuel Filter (Optional Accessory)			X		
	Replace Spark Plug				X	
	Clean Combustion Chamber Deposits					X

* Change oil after first 5 hours of use, then every 50 hours or every season.

**Clean more often under dusty conditions or when airborne debris is present. Replace air-cleaner parts if very dirty.

MISCELLANEOUS NOTES

NOTES

NOTES

NOTES

NOTES

A

Acceleration problems, possible causes, 50
AC volts test, 105-106
Air cleaner assembly,
  and safety, 13
  attaching, 97
  maintenance schedule, 43, 45, 52
  servicing, 52-55
  shown on diagram, 16, 18
  troubleshooting, 61
  types of air cleaners, 53
Air flow, 29
Air-fuel mixture in carburetor,
  screws to regulate, 25
  throttle and air flow, 25
Air guides, 29
Air plenum, 29
Air vane, 28, 30
Alternating current vs. direct
  current, 35
Alternator, 34-35, 104
  testing, 104-105
Altitude, compensating for high
  altitude, 96
Aluminum engine, RPM
  recommendation, 78
Anti-afterfire solenoid, 92-93
Automobile engine compared to small
  engine, 14

B

Battery, 33
  charging system, 34-35
  connections, 13
  safety, 105
Blower housing, 29
  and safety, 13
  cleaning, 67-68
  maintenance schedule, 43, 45
  shown on diagram, 16-18
Brake adjustment gauge, 130
Brake bail, 122
Brake band or pad, 32-33, 122
  inspecting and testing brake pad
    system, 124
  removing and inspecting band
    brake, 126
  removing brake pad, 123
  testing and adjusting band
    brake, 127
  when to adjust, 122
  when to replace, 124
Brake bracket, 32-33
Brake cover, 32
Braking system, 14, 32-33
  cleaning, 68
  diagram of parts, 33
  flywheel brake, 14-15, 99
  removing band brake, 126
  servicing band brake system,
    126-127
  servicing brake pad system, 122-125
  shown on diagram, 15
Breaker point ignition systems, 27,
  100
  retrofitting with solid-state ignition,
    100, 102-103
  troubleshooting, 61
Briggs, Steve, 6-7
Briggs & Stratton, contacting, 5
Bypass valve, 29

C

Cables, lubricating, 57
Capacitor, 34
Carbon deposits,
  possible causes of, 46, 61
  removing, 108-111
Carburetor,
  adjusting, 76-79
  attaching, 97
  cleaning, 90-97
  diagram of parts, 25, 91
  disassembling, 93-95
  gumming up by unstabilized
    gasoline, 44, 116
  how carburetor works, 14-15, 25
  inspecting, 95-96
  maintenance schedule, 43-44
  reassembling, 97
  removing, 92
  shown on diagram, 15-16, 18, 25
  troubleshooting, 60-61, 77, 82
  when to adjust, 60, 90
Carburetor jet screwdriver, 130
Cast-iron engine, RPM
  recommendation, 78
Charging system, see: Electrical
  system
Chemicals and safety, 13
Choke, 24, 95
  adjusting choke linkage, 79
  choke parts shown on diagram,
    25, 91
  disassembling, 94
  reassembling, 97
  troubleshooting, 60, 77
Cobalite™ exhaust valves, 117
Combustion chamber, 22
  importance of seal, 20
  maintenance schedule, 44
  shown on diagram, 15, 21, 23
Compression stroke, 22
Compression system, 20-23
  diagram of parts, 21
  explanation of four-stroke cycle, 22
  function of compression system,
    14-15, 20
  maintenance schedule, 43
  problems, 21, 57
  testing compression, 56-57
Compressor, 9
Connecting rod,
  function of, 21
  shown on diagram, 21
  troubleshooting, 60
Cooling fins, 28-29
  cleaning, 67
  maintenance schedule, 43
  shown on diagram, 15, 29
Cooling system, 14-15, 28-29
  diagram of parts, 29
  maintenance schedule, 43
  role of oil in cooling, 28
Crankcase, 28
  and temperature regulation, 14
  shown on diagram, 17, 19
Crankcase breather, 56
  inspecting and maintenance, 57
  removing to access valves, 114
Crank, governor, 30-31
Crankshaft,
  crankshaft and governor
    relationship, 30
  how crankshaft works, 14-15, 21, 26
  shown on diagram, 15-19, 21, 81
C-ring installation tool, 130
C-ring removal tool, 130
Customer service,
  Briggs & Stratton, 5
Cutting screen, 29
Cylinder,
  cylinder block, 29
  cylinder head, 16-20, 29
  decarbonizing cylinder head, 43,
    108-111
  deposits on head, possible causes, 50
  function of cylinder, 21
  maintenance schedule, 43, 45
  reassembling cylinder head, 111
  removing cylinder head and
    bolts, 109
  shown on diagram, 15-19, 21
  troubleshooting, 60
Cylinder leakdown tester, 130

D

DC amps test, 105-106
DC shunt, 130
Debris, 66
  and safety, 63, 65
  inspecting for, 67
  removing, 43, 45, 61, 67-69, 77
Degreasing engine, 69
Detergent oil, 47
Dipper, 28
Dipstick, 28-29
  how to check oil with dipstick, 47

shown on diagram, 16-19
Direct current vs. alternating
  current, 35
Drain plug, 28, 48
Dusty conditions,
  air cleaners for, 52-53
  and maintenance schedule, 43, 46

E

Ear protection, 13
Electrical system, 14, 34-35
  alternating current vs. direct
    current, 35
  testing electrical components,
    104-107
Electric starter, 14
  battery connections, 13
Emissions and two-stroke engines, 23
  how to reduce, 37, 44
Emulsion tube,
  removing, 95
  shown on diagram, 25, 91
Engine efficiency,
  and overhead valve design, 23
  factors that affect, 20, 112
Engine speed,
  adjusting fuel mixtures, 78-79
  and governor system, 30-31, 80
  engine speed control shown on
    diagram, 81
  factors that affect, 30, 66
  hunting and surging, 82
  setting top no-load speed, 85
  slowdown, possible causes of, 52, 66
  see also: Governor system; Speed
    control
Engine stops suddenly, possible
  cause, 69
Engine temperature,
  how it is regulated, 14
Exhaust stroke, 22
Exhaust valves, 113
  function of exhaust valves, 22, 113
  shown on diagram, 15-19, 21
  see also: Valves and valve parts
Extended-life air filter, 53
Eye protection, 13, 118

F

Face mask, 13
Feeler gauge, 57
Filters,
  air filter, 38, 43, 45, 52-55, 61
  fuel filter, 25, 70-73
  oil filter, 28-29, 43, 46, 48
Fins, see: Cooling fins; Flywheel fins
Fire prevention, 12-13
Flathead design, 20
Float and float bowl, 95

adjusting, 78
  maintenance schedule, 43-44
  reassembling, 97
  removing, 93
  shown on diagram, 25, 91
  when to adjust, 60
Flooded engine,
  starting, 12
  troubleshooting, 60
Flyer, 6
Flyweights, 30-31
  shown on diagram, 81
Flywheel, 26
  and safety, 13, 99
  braking system for, 7, 14-11, 18, 99
  checking compression, 56-57
  cleaning, 67
  flywheel magnets in electrical
    system, 34
  function of flywheel, 98
  inspecting, 98-99
  installing, 99
  lubricating cables and linkages in
    brake, 57
  removing, 99
  shown on diagram, 16-19, 27
  troubleshooting, 61
Flywheel fins, 28-29
  cleaning, 67
  function of fins, 98
Flywheel key,
  function of flywheel key, 98
  inspecting, 98-99
  replacing, 99
  troubleshooting, 60-61
Flywheel strap wrench, 130
Four-stroke engine,
  and safety, 12-13
  determining if engine is four-
    stroke, 73
  engine components, 15
  explanation of four-stroke cycle, 22
  how engines work, 14-15
  parts, 16-19
  starting, 12, 14
Fuel bowl, 25, 60
Fuel consumption,
  possible causes of excess, 50, 114
  reducing, 37
Fuel filter, 25, 70-71, 77
  servicing, 72-73
Fuel line, 24-25
  maintenance schedule, 43
  shown on diagram, 25
  troubleshooting, 60
Fuel pump, 24-25, 77
  servicing, 74-75
Fuel stabilizer, 38, 44, 73
Fuel system, 14, 24-25
  diagram of parts, 25
  servicing fuel filter, 72-73

servicing fuel pump, 74-75
  servicing fuel tank, 70-71
  troubleshooting, 60-61, 77
Fuel tank, 24-25
  labyrinth device, 71
  maintenance schedule, 43
  removing and cleaning, 70-71
  shown on diagram, 16-19
  troubleshooting, 60-61
Fuel valve, 60, 77

G

Gapping spark plug, 26-27, 60-61
Garden tiller, see: Tiller
Gasket, leaky, 61
Gasoline,
  adding oil to gasoline, 61, 73
  gasoline use tips, 73
  safety, 13
  stabilizing for off-season storage, 44
  unleaded gasoline to reduce carbon
    deposits, 108
  using old gasoline in automobile, 73
Generator, see: Portable generator
Gloves for working on small
  engines, 13
Governor system, 30-31
  adjusting, 80-85
  cleaning, 68
  debris in governor system, 66, 68
  diagrams of parts, 31, 81
  how governor works, 14, 30, 80
  inspecting, 82
  lubricating cables and linkages, 57
  maintenance schedule, 43
  shown on diagram, 15
  static governor adjustment, 82-83
  troubleshooting, 82
  types of governor settings, 84

H

High altitude,
  compensating for, 96
High speed mixture, adjusting, 79
History of small engines, 6-7
Hunting and surging, 82
Hydraulic lift, 9

I

Idle speed and idle mixture screws,
  adjusting governed idle, 84
  adjusting idle speed mixture, 78
  removing idle mixture screw and
    spring, 94
  shown on diagram, 25, 91
Ignition armature, 26, 100
  common gap ranges, 101
  installing and adjusting, 101

maintenance schedule, 43
removing, 101
replacing, 100-103
shown on diagram, 15, 17, 19, 27
troubleshooting, 60
Ignition system, 14, 26-27
diagram of parts, 27
maintenance schedule, 43
replacing the ignition, 100-103
solid-state, 61
troubleshooting, 61
Inlet needle, 97
Intake stroke, 22
Intake valves, 113
function of intake valves, 15, 20, 22, 113
shown on diagram, 15-19, 21
see also: Valves and valve parts
Intek (OHV), 118
Internal combustion engine, how internal combustion works, 14

J

Jet,
adjusting, 78-79
carburetor jet screwdriver, 130
high-altitude adjustments, 96
shown on diagram, 25, 91

K

Key, see: Flywheel key
Keyhole retainers,
reinstalling, 118
removing, 115
Kill switch, troubleshooting, 60
Knocking,
and octane of gasoline, 73
possible causes, 21, 108

L

Labyrinth device for fuel tank, 71
Lapping valves, 112, 117
valve lapping tool, 130
Lawnmower,
maintenance, 37-39
oil, 49
Leakdown tester clamp, 130
Leaks,
around fuel cap, 70
around valves or rings, 57
L-head design, 20
diagram, 113
valve location, 113
Linkages,
adjusting choke linkage, 79
cleaning, 68
governor system, 30-31, 82
inspecting, 82
lubricating, 57
maintenance schedule, 43
Load,

and maintenance schedule, 43
role of governor in engine performance, 80
Lubricating cables and linkages, 57
Lubrication and lubrication system, 28-29
basic principles, 14-15
before off-season storage, 44-45
how to check and change oil and filter, 46-49

M

Magnets, 26, 98, 100
in electrical system, 34
shown on diagram, 15, 27
Maintenance of small engines, 42-57
and safety, 13
kits, 37, 39
schedule, 43-45
March is Mower Tune-Up Month, 37
Mechanical governor, 30-31
diagram of parts, 81
see also: Governor system
Miss, see: Spark plug miss
Mixture screws, inspecting, 96
Model P, 7
Mounting bolts, tightening, 57
Mower, see: Lawnmower
Muffler, 62
and safety, 12, 62-63, 65-66
how muffler works, 63
inspecting and changing, 64-65
maintenance schedule, 43, 45
removing rusty muffler, 65
removing to access valves, 114
shown on diagram, 16, 18
Multi-viscosity oil, 28-29

N

Noises made by engine, possible causes,
decrease in engine sound, 51
excessive noise, 62
popping sound, 51

O

Octane rating of gasoline for small engines, 73
OHV, *see:* Overhead valve engine
Oil,
adding oil to gasoline, 61, 73
characteristics and grades, 28, 47
checking, 43, 46-47
disposal of used oil, 48
function in small engine, 28
how to change, 48-49
oil dilution, possible causes, 50
possible cause of excessive oil consumption, 108
proper amount of oil, 46
removing old, 49

synthetic, 47, 49
types, 49
when to change, 38, 43-44, 46
see also: Lubrication and lubrication system
Oil dipper, 28
Oil evacuation pump, 49
Oil fill cap, 16-17, 19, 28, 47
Oil seal protectors, 130
Oil slinger, 28
shown on diagram, 29
Overhead valve engine, 16-17, 20, 23
adjusting overhead valves, 121
diagram, 16-17, 113
installing overhead valves, 120
removing overhead valves for servicing, 119
valve location, 113
Overheating engine,
possible causes, 108
troubleshooting, 61, 66

P

Pinging, causes, 21
Piston ring compressor, 130
Piston ring expander, 130
Piston rings, 21
shown on diagram, 21
Pistons,
explanation of four-stroke cycle, 22
how pistons work, 14-15, 20-21
shown on diagram, 15-19, 21
troubleshooting, 60
Plenum, see: Air plenum
Plug gauge, 130
Pneumatic governor, 30-31, 66, 98
cleaning, 68
see also: Governor system
Points, troubleshooting, 60
Popping sound, possible causes, 51
Portable generator, 9
Power loss, possible causes of, 52, 66
Power stroke, 22
Pre-cleaner for air cleaner system, 52-53
servicing, 55
Primer, 16
Push rods, 113
shown on diagram, 23, 113

Q

Quantum engine, about, 7

R

Raptor engine, about, 7
Recoil system, 86
Rectifier, 34-35, 106
Regulator, 34-35, 106
Replacement parts, 13, 27, 129
Rewind and rewind cord, 14, 26
how rewind cord works, 26

maintenance schedule, 43
  shown on diagram, 15-19
  testing and replacing, 86-87
Rewind tool, 130
Rings, leaks around, 57
Rocker arms, 20
  shown on diagram, 23, 113
Rotator, 112
RPM recommendations for small
  engines, 78
Rusty muffler, removing, 65

S

Safety and small engines, 12-13
  battery, 105
  braking system, 32
  flywheel, 13, 99
  fuel system, 70
  rewind starting system, 87
Safety shoes, 13
Seasonal maintenance, 43-45, 66
Shut-off procedure, 12-13
  see also: Braking system; Stop
    switch
Smoke, possible causes of, 46, 51, 61
Socket wrenches, 56
  spark plug socket, 50-51
Solenoid, anti-afterfire, 92-93
Solid-state ignition, 61
  photo of various types, 102
  retrofitting breaker point ignition
    system with solid state, 100,
    102-103
Solvent, working with, 92, 110
Soot around muffler, 62, 64
  checking for soot inside muffler, 65
Sound of engine, see: Noises made by
  engine
Spark arrester, 12
Spark plug, 26, 38
  and safety, 13
  cleaning, 51
  explanation of four-stroke cycle, 22
  function of spark plugs, 14-15
  inspecting, 51
  maintenance schedule, 43, 45, 50
  servicing, 50-51
  shown on diagram, 15-17, 19, 27
  spark plug lead, 26-27
  troubleshooting, 60-61, 77
Spark plug gauge, using, 51
Spark miss,
  checking for, 51
  possible causes of, 50, 61
Spark plug socket, 50-51
Spark tester, 60
  using, 51
Speed control, 14, 30
  see also: Governor system
Stabilizer for gasoline, 38, 44, 73
Starter clutch wrench, 130
Starter system, 15, 104

Starting problems, troubleshooting,
  59-60
Starting small engines,
  and safety, 12
  causes of difficult starting, 50,
    59-60, 77, 104
  how small engines work, 14-15
Static governor, 82
  setting, 83
Stator, 34, 104
  adjusting air gap, 107
  replacing, 106-107
Stop switch, 32, 122
  checking and reattaching, 69
  installing, 125
  shown on diagram, 15, 33
  testing, 101
Stratton, Harry, 6-7
Stroke diagrams, 22
Synthetic oil, 47, 49

T

Tachometer,
  using to adjust engine RPM, 78, 85
  using to test alternator, 106
Tang bending tool, 10
Tappets, 113
  adjusting tappet clearance, 117
Telescoping gauge, 130
Temperature, see: Engine
  temperature
Throat in carburetor, 25
Throttle, 25, 95
  disassembling, 94
  lubricating cables and linkages, 57
  reassembling, 97
  role of governor in throttle
    adjustment, 30, 80
  throttle parts shown on diagram,
    25, 81, 91
Tiller, 9
Timing, 26
  how four-stroke engines work, 14
Toll-free telephone number, Briggs &
  Stratton, 5
Tools for small engine repair,
  10-11, 40, 130
Torque wrench, 130
Transporting small engines,
  and safety, 13
Troubleshooting, 59-61
Trowel, walk-behind, 9
Tune-up, 37-38
Two-stroke engine, 23

V

Valve lapping tool, 130
Valve retainer, 112-121
Valve rotator, 117
Valves and valve parts,
  adjusting overhead valves, 121
  adjusting tappet clearance, 117

diagrams of valve design, 113
  extending valve life, 117
  how valves work, 14-15, 20, 112-113
  inspecting, 110, 112, 116
  installing overhead valves, 120
  lapping, 117
  leaks around valves, 57
  machining, 114
  maintenance schedule, 43
  reinstalling, 118
  removing, 114-115, 119
  removing carbon from valve
    parts, 110
  replacing seat inserts, 117
  safety when working with
    springs, 118
  servicing, 112-121
  shown on diagram, 15-19, 21,
    23, 113
  troubleshooting, 60-61, 116
  tuning up, 112
  when to replace valve components,
    116-117
Valve spring compressor, 114
  using, 115, 118
Ventilation and safety, 12
Venturi, 77
  shown on diagram, 91
Vibration,
  correcting, 57
  effect on small engines, 56

W

Washing machine, gas-powered, 7
Weather and engine maintenance,
  43, 46
Website,
  Briggs & Stratton, 5, 41
  National Mower Tune-Up Month, 37
Welch plug, 91, 97
Wire connections,
  troubleshooting, 60
Wood chipper, 9